Mr. Metcalfe's

Congre Chapel at Roxton

PUBLISHED BY GUILDEN PRESS FOR
ROXTON CONGREGATIONAL CHURCH
TO MARK THE BICENTENNIAL
2008

Text: Copyright Stella Gibbs 2008

We have made every effort to trace the current copyright owners of all the photographs we have used. Any errors that may have occurred are inadvertent and the author welcomes notification of corrections.

© All rights reserved. No part of this book may be reproduced without prior permission of the copyright holder in writing.

ISBN 978-1-898024-20-0

Designed and Printed by
DESIGN TO PRINT LIMITED
46 Daventry Road, Norton, Daventry, NN11 2ND

'Go and tell my servant David, thus saith the Lord shalt thou build me an house for me to dwell in'
2 Samuel : 7 : 5

Roxton Chapel viewed from the south; Steve Eldridge

THIS BOOK IS DEDICATED TO ALL THOSE WHO HAVE
SERVED THE LORD GOD IN THIS CHURCH AND
THE MANY WHO HAVE WORSHIPPED HERE THROUGHOUT
TWO HUNDRED YEARS

Charles James Metcalfe - founder : D. Fox Collection

Acknowledgements

The Deacons or Roxton Congregational Church gratefully acknowledge the generous financial support given by the following to offset the costs of publishing this history.

Corporate Bodies & Local Organisations
Lafarge Aggregates
Npower, Little Barford Power Station
Roxton and District Local History Group
Roxton Parish Council
St. Neots United Reformed Church
Bunyan Meeting Free Church

Members and Friends of the Church
Mrs. M. Bambridge
Mr. S. Bath
Elisabeth Cromwell, Ian Gosling & Sheila Verrier in remembrance of their parents, Marjorie & Philip Gosling
Mr. & Mrs. J Gibbs
Mr. & Mrs. B. Hooker
Mr. R. Hooker
Mrs. C. Haines
Mrs. D. Jefferies
Mr. & Mrs. R. Randall
Mr. &. Mrs. P. Wood

The author wishes to acknowledge the help given in the preparation of this work by:
Bedford and Luton Archives and Records Service, (hereafter called B.L.A.R.S.); the staff & the archive website.
Cambridgeshire Archives Service, Huntingdon, & the staff.
St. Neots United Reformed Church.
Roxton Women's Institute, for permission to include photographs from their 1958 Village Scrapbook
Mr. Steve Eldridge, for taking responsibility for special photography and reprographics.
Dianne Fox, for Metcalfe family genealogy and anecdotal notes.
All who have contributed photographs and helped in any other way with research.

Contents

Front Cover: Roxton Congregational Church Summer 2007, featuring Mr. R. Metcalfe of New Zealand, 3 x Great Grandson of the founder.   *Stella Gibbs*

Back Cover: Engraving of a drawing by Mrs E. Metcalfe of the church in 1808.

i	*Dedication*
ii	*Acknowledgements*
iii	*Contents*
1	Introduction
4	Foreword
5	Chapter 1: The Metcalfe Family and Roxton House.
13	Chapter 2: The Early Church.
30	Chapter 3: A Period of Growth 1835-1851.
43	Chapter 4: Difficult Times.
55	Chapter 5: The Metcalfe Family: a Postscript.
61	Chapter 6: The Early 20th Century.
74	Men Commemorated on the Congregational Church Roll of Honour.
80	Chapter 7: Twenty Years of Faithful Leadership.
96	Chapter 8: An Era of Change 1945-1980
115	Chapter 9: The Closing Years of the Millennium.
125	Chapter 10: Into the 21st Century.
130	Appendix 1: Pastors and Ministers.
131	Appendix 2: Some who Served in This Church
133	Appendix 3: Marriages.
136	Index.

Introduction

The approach of the bicentenary of Roxton Congregational Church, with all that such an anniversary implies, seemed to be the right time for the writing of a new and up-to-date history. The previous, well researched history by H.G.Tibbutt, published in 1958 for the One Hundred and Fiftieth Anniversary and so long out of print, lacked the visual content that today's printing technology can produce. Much material is available; church records are still held at the church with the exception of the church book that spans the years 1873-1908 which seems to have been missing for very many years. Many images are also available, simply because the rustic charm and rural setting of the church hold appeal to photographer and artist alike, and members have collections of old photographs passed down by former generations.

Any church history that begins as you enter the door cannot tell a complete story. The story of a church is so much more; it is the story of the people whose faith and ideals spurred them to found the church and of the community that responded to use and maintain it ever since. In the case of Roxton the founding of the Congregational Church was the outcome of the exceptional faith of one man and his family, a family that fate chose to remove from the midst of his Christian friends and the village during his lifetime. The story of the Metcalfe family of Roxton has faded from village consciousness, while their Chapel has become part of the identity of the place, but Metcalfe's had influence in Roxton for over one hundred and fifty years and their story, briefly told here, sets the scene for this history of Charles James Metcalfe's Roxton 'Barn Chapel'.

I have attempted to relate something of outside events and movements that had influence over both the development of this church and the village community that worshipped here. In various ways the following would have held important influence; the development of the Bedfordshire Union of Christians as a means of support for small rural churches; concerns for community cohesion as identified by the Anglican Clergy, arising from the inception of the Independent movement in the County; the condition of the rural poor, low wages and a lack of schooling; the difficulties faced by this church without financial support and at times lacking leadership; wars and their aftermaths; social stagnation or mobility, and finally, in more recent times the changing face of village community coupled with a general decline in the numbers attending all traditional forms of Christian worship.

The pages tell of inspirational spiritual leaders and of generations of village people, many from the same families, whose devoted, often lifelong service has been directed to maintain worship here and who have constantly, generously supported the upkeep of this extremely costly building. The story told here then is of a church fellowship and the building in which it worshipped. It is a story that includes something of the wider support offered by local sister church communities, as well as something of aspects of the wider ecumenical fellowship that have been and are shared in this area of North Bedfordshire.

Since I come from a family that has been connected with the Church for many years, I was pleased to be given the responsibility of writing this history. In so doing I have referred to the church records and recollections of church members that have lain unread since I collected them twenty or more years ago. Conscious of the huge responsibility I trust that my efforts have resulted in a true record that will stand for many subsequent years. One of the delights of this project has been that of new friends made. I am now in regular contact with Metcalfe family members in New Zealand and Australia. The cover photograph is of Mr. R. Metcalfe, direct descendent of the founder, who visited Roxton from New Zealand in the Summer of 2007.

Due to the generous sponsorship received for this publication which has almost covered costs of printing, sales of this book will contribute to the upkeep of the church building, and the continuation of worship at Roxton Congregational Church into the 21st Century.

My thanks are due to all who have contributed in any way to this publication. I am grateful to Margaret Bambridge and Doris Jefferies for their memories and recollections as well as to the many people who willingly agreed to be interviewed in the past and who now are sadly are no longer with us; Marjorie Gosling, George Arthur Bambridge, Margaret Robinson, Louis Livett and Gwendoline Gadsden. They were all a delight to talk to some twenty or so years ago. Most of them like my late grandparents Florence and Thomas Bambridge and great aunt and uncle, Elizabeth and Frederick Gilbert, grew up in the church and were able to tell me of their parents' time in the church fellowship. For images and photographs thanks are also due to the many who have given permission for their family photographs to be reproduced here and to Roxton W.I for permission to reproduce pictures from their 1956 Scrapbook; to Steve Eldridge, who was helped by his enthusiastic family; and my husband who has promised to re-educate me in the art of cooking and housework in the near future.

Stella Gibbs, March 2008

~ ~ ~ ~ ~ ~ ~ ~ ~ ~ ~ ~ ~ ~ ~

Members and friends assembling with Rev. and Mrs. K.Trice before the Harvest Service, September 2007; *S. Gibbs.*

Foreword

It may help the reader to bear these points in mind when reading the text.

The Church Name and Christian Leaders

The Independent Church movement is explained elsewhere, but it is an assembly of Christians who wished to worship freely in a way that was other than that prescribed by the Anglican Church. The Congregational Church was one of the denominations or different categories of Independent Churches.

The early church leaders of the Independent movement were generally known as Pastors. Many were trained at Independent Colleges where they studied classics and divinity. Later trained non-conformist clergy were generally known as Ministers.

Worship in the Building at Roxton began at a time when most such Independent meeting buildings or 'houses' were called Meeting Houses. (Bunyan Meeting, Bedford, retains that name today.) The Roxton building, having previously been a barn, was apparently referred to as The Barn Chapel, Roxton in its early days. To begin with I have referred to it in general terms as a meeting house, and later in general terms as a church. Specifically I refer to it as the Church or the Chapel, but always this means the Church as the subject of this book. Over time, village people have come to call it simply *The Chapel*, to differentiate it from the Anglican Church, which in like manner is simply called *The Church*. The modern name is The Congregational Church, Roxton.

Often the term 'Fellowship' was used to denote the assemblage of people that comprised a church who met at a given place.

The Metcalfe Family

They were typical in naming two generations with the same Christian name. Hence we have to distinguish between Charles senior and Charles Junior. I have done this by referring to Charles senior as Charles James Metcalfe or Charles Metcalfe Esq. whilst Charles Junior simply as Charles Metcalfe.

Notes

I have annotated some points to further help any reader who wishes to consult my sources. Notes appear at the chapter ends. I ask those intent on reading for pleasure to simply ignore the embedded numbers.

The Metcalfe Family of Roxton House.

A history of a church is necessarily bound up with the history of the community that it serves. The Chapel at Roxton more so because of the family who founded it and their unique association with the village. The Metcalfe family, long forgotten, were Lords of the Manor in Roxton, farmed extensively around the village and lived at Roxton Park. It is therefore relevant to briefly cite their historical connection with the village and the people here, before going on to tell about Charles James Metcalfe, founder and third generation of the family. His high Independent Christian ideals, and enormous financial commitment, brought about the development of this Church and enabled so many to worship in the way they chose throughout two hundred years.

Setting the Scene

We learn from the returns, or reports about the Parish, made by the Vicar, John Rewse to the Bishop of Lincoln in 1706, that there was, 'No Gentleman of Estate' living in the Parish.[1] He goes on to report that neither was there a 'Publick or Charity School'. Consequently it was left to the Anglican clergy to do what they could for the parishioners. Reporting again in 1717 Rev. Rewse stated that he privately taught some children, 'the principles of the Church of England'.[2] We can assume that the majority of the inhabitants of the Parish were extremely poor and ill-educated and that there was little help for the sick and the old, other than meagre handouts made by the Guardians of the Poor under the Old Poor Law, to any who were in desperate need.[3] There was no recorded Poor House in the village.

Life was to change slowly after the Metcalfe family became owners of major tracts of land at both Roxton and Gt. Barford at some time between 1687 and 1717. Their properties and holdings at Roxton were the Manorial land and the house at Roxton Park. Roxton Farm was nearby with stables, cowsheds and barns including the Great Tithe Barn. The house was sited within a park of 36 acres and along with woods and fishing rights on three miles of the nearby river Ouse they held five other farms on the Roxton Manor holding. Their estate also comprised of Netherbury Manor farm at Gt. Barford, Chawston Manor farm and Chawston House estate.[4] It is feasible that the moated Manor House at Chawston was acquired at approximately the same time. Mary Hunt, spinster, is named as the last member of the Hunt family to own the Manor, in 1705.[5] The Metcalfe family at this time owned property at Fordham, Cambridgeshire where they chose to reside.

Trinity College, Cambridge was the other holder of considerable acreage and since the college held patronage of the living of St. Mary Magdalene the Anglican Church, it also held influence over the lives of the village community.

James Metcalfe Acquires Land at Roxton

The Metcalfe family are first recorded in Madras, India where Captain Charles Metcalfe served and made his home. His son James Metcalfe Esq. had been born in Madras, India in 1686 and was the first Metcalfe to own land and property at Roxton which was bought from William de Laune.[6] It is possible that James lived at the Roxton house as landowner and Lord of the Manor, although at that time it would not have been an essential requisite when he stood as a parliamentary candidate in 1727. In this he was supported by the third Duke of Bedford, who was a Whig. Having successfully challenged his opponent's conduct in the election he was appointed to represent the Borough of Bedford in Parliament, a position he held until his death. He had married, a Mary (Benson), and the couple had three daughters, Mary, Sarah and Caroline, but apparently no son. Although he died at Roxton and was buried there on December 4th 1730, no memorial marks his burial place.

William Metcalfe, younger brother of James, was also born in India, but came to England for his education. He graduated from Trinity College, Oxford in 1713 at the age of 16 years before returning at some time to join his family in India. Metcalfe family history records indicate that he returned to England immediately after his older brother's death to assume ownership of the Roxton manorial title and property. Although it was to Fordham that he returned, it was obviously necessary for him to take over the running of the Roxton estate. He may have lived part of the time at the old house at Roxton Park, adjacent to the old tithe barn, but was married to Catherine (Affleck) at Fordham. There is no entry in the Fordham registers of the birth of their children, first Catherine, then James and Charlotte, so it is possible that the family did live at Roxton in the early years of their married life. William and Catherine had seven children and since the baptisms of the last four are recorded at Fordham we can assume that the family were living there between 1743 and William's death in 1785. Records for Fordham show that the old Abbey had been demolished some time earlier by a previous owner who had rebuilt the manor house. However that house too lacked the modern comforts expected by the Metcalfe family and it was most likely to have been William who pulled that house down to replace it with a brick house, before settling there for the last forty or so years of his life.[7]

Nevertheless records show that manorial courts were held at Roxton in William's name and even though he was often an absentee landlord, he would have retained a considerable influence over the little community at Roxton, since many of the villager labourers were, after all, reliant on him for their employment and wages.

Living at Fordham, however, meant that he would have been a remote figure. It was a long ride by carriage or on horseback and no doubt he let the Roxton estate run itself under the direction of an agent, who would have overseen the farms and properties and collected rents from the tenants. His will dated 27th October 1778 confirms that he was 'of Fordham Abbey'.

James, the first son to be born to William and Catherine in 1742 inherited the Estate and title on the death of his father in 1785, when he was 43 years old. He had married Susanna (Banyard) at St. Paul's, Covent Garden, Westminster in that same year. James and Susanna were forced to live at Roxton in the old house at Roxton Park, but family records indicate that it was not their first choice. James had unfortunately been forced to sell the property at Fordham. Metcalfe family anecdotal history *suggests* that the sale may have been forced to meet debts incurred at Newmarket. James is said to have been angry at having to come and live in the house at Roxton, which he described as a *kennel*.[8]

A New House is Built at Roxton

It may have been James who pulled down the old house and built a new red brick house at Roxton Park some time towards the end of the 18th century. Illustrations exist showing the original house and it is said that the new house was erected on the same site. The old house was said to face east whereas the new one was turned to face almost north.

James Metcalfe died at Roxton at the age of fifty one, only eight years after he inherited the estate. He was buried in the chancel of the church of St. Mary Magdelene, Roxton, where a memorial in Latin, on the south wall, commemorates his life. Erected by his wife who was many years his junior and survived him by fifty-six years, the memorial describes him as 'Arms bearer of this parish'. In his will which, was proved in July 1793, he is described as being 'of Roxton House, Bedfordshire'.

Charles James Metcalfe was born to James Metcalfe and Susanna (Banyard), his wife, in 1786 and was baptised at Fordham. He was their second but only surviving son; however there were three daughters, Sophia, Frances and Susanna, born previously to their mother. These girls, who were said to be illegitimate, were brought up in the Metcalfe household at Roxton as the older sisters of Charles James. On his father's death Charles was a boy of six years. It was not until he came of age in 1807 that he was able to assume authority over the estate that he inherited.

Charles married Elizabeth May of Maulden in Essex in 1813. When the young couple aged 21 and 18 years came to reside at the house at Roxton, Susanna his mother, with her two unmarried daughters Sophia and Frances moved to live at Chawston Manor. In James's will provision had been made for the living expenses of his wife Susanna and his two unmarried step-daughters, which was to place a continuing financial burden on the estate since they were to be dependent on the estate for very many years. Charles and Elizabeth, according to family tradition, were quite unmindful of the responsibilities of running an estate or of ensuring the security of the family finances. Here, in Roxton, they seemingly brought up their young family in blissful happiness. Both were connected with nonconformity; Elizabeth May it is said came from a family who were staunch Independents, and the practice of their Christian faith was an integral part of their family life. In time the couple were to have a significant influence on the development and growth of Christian worship in this small rural community.

The new house at Roxton Park, built c.1800, showing proximity to the site of the Barn Chapel   *S. Eldridge*

As befitted their status, they would have kept quite a large household. The house with its stables, coach-house, barns and outbuildings along with a walled garden, and complete with a laundry, dairy and even a brew-house, would call for many hands to run it. [9]

There would have been the usual household servants, maids, cook housekeeper and with a band of growing children, probably a nursemaid and a tutor to take responsibility for their education.

Worship at St. Neots

Charles and Elizabeth resolutely dissented from worship at the village Anglican Church. Choosing to worship with other non-conformists, the family, accompanied by their servants, made the difficult journey to St. Neots regularly on Sunday mornings to attend the service at the Old Meeting church. (This church was situated behind where the present United Reformed Church is sited). The list of members of the St. Neots Old Meeting begins in the year 1791, but that church grew out of an even earlier Meeting of Dissenters that was formed at Hail Weston village in 1691. It is suggested that from the Hail Weston church, a new group of worshippers emerged, who, being centred on St. Neots, found it appropriate to separate and start their own Meeting. [10]

St Neots Old Meeting c.1800   *Cambridge Archives, Huntingdon, FR 16/8/2*

Among the records of St. Neots Old Meeting is a book dated 1812, which is titled the 'Pew Register and Account Book'. It records the annual payment made by members for the pews in which they always sat. It was the practise of churches to gain regular financial support in this way. This record shows that Charles Metcalfe paid for several rows of seats, which were known by numbers.

For pew No. 13 he paid 18 guineas; this was by far the most expensive pew rent in the building rent and hence we must assume that the pew was most advantageously placed. It was marked for Mr. Metcalfe and family. He also paid 12 guineas for the five seats in pew No. 20, and four seats in pew No. 21 presumably for his Mother and Sisters. The amounts paid were extremely generous and far exceed the amount paid by others. Additionally more seats in pew 51 were earmarked for Mr. Metcalfe's servants as well as two further rows of five seats each for each of which he paid two sums of £1-4s-00. We learn that nearby seats in pews 49 and 50 were reserved for the singers.[11]

St. Neots Old Meeting Account Book, showing Charles James Metcalfe as a signatory, possibly as treasurer. Cambridge Archives, Huntingdon FR 16/5/1

It is not easy for us to imagine the difficulties of travelling in the early 18th century. Road surfaces were of compacted mud with gravel used to repair them. They became rutted and extremely muddy during wet weather. Coaches travelled relatively slowly; it was reckoned that a chaise and four (horses) could travel at ten miles an hour, or a chaise and two at seven miles an hour. It would therefore have taken about an hour to get the travellers on board and cover the distance to church at St.Neots. Given that sermons were much longer then and could sometimes last an hour, we can conclude that the trip to St. Neots possibly meant the Metcalfe's were away from home for near enough four hours. The Metcalfe contingent, complete with servants and Susanna and her two daughters are likely to have filled three carriages for the journey to Sunday worship.

Their association with the St. Neots Meeting spanned a relatively short time; it seems to have begun when the young couple took up residence at Roxton, was associated with Charles' Sister Susannah's marriage to Rev. Morelle, and lasted until 1822 when records show them leaving to take up regular worship at Roxton.

Services at St. Neots were supported by leaders of the Bedford Union of Christians. This body was instrumental in supporting the burgeoning Independent church movement throughout Bedfordshire, although the St. Neots Old Meeting Church, in Huntingdonshire was included in its membership. Records indicate that Charles Metcalfe was probably one of the St. Neots church elders and thus he would have met men of influence in the Bedford Union movement. He was also involved in arranging for a new pastor, Rev. James Morell to take up the St. Neots pastorate.

Rev. T. Morell, Pastor at St. Neots Old Meeting 1802-1821 Cambridge Archives, Huntingdon FR16/8/2

Rev. Morell first preached in January 1802 and was subsequently invited to accept the pastorate; it was Mr. Metcalfe who wrote to confirm his appointment. James Morelle was married to Susanna, one of Charles Metcalfe's half-sisters. His ministry at St. Neots lasted nearly nineteen years during which, the records state, 'the congregation greatly increased'. He left in June 1822 to take up a position at Wymondley Academical Institution in Hertfordshire, where he was to tutor students for the Independent ministry.

Notes

1. Patricia Bell (ed.) *Episcopal Visitations in Bedfordshire 1706-1720*, B.H.R.S. Vol.81, 2002. p.75.

2. *ibid* p. 161

3. B.L.A.R.S., Roxton Overseers of the Poor Books 1683-1839 (incomplete) P28/11/1, P28/12/1-9, P28/12/10

4. www.bedfordshire.gov.uk/archive, Community archive: Chawston: Chawston House.

5. *ibid*.

6. Victoria County History, Vol. 2. Manors p.219 note 28. B.L.A.R.S.

7. See Vision of Britain website, Imperial Gazetteer of England and Wales; 1870-72. Fordham, Cambridgeshire. John Marius Wilson

8. Anecdotal Metcalfe family history. Ms. Dianne Fox.

9. B.L.A.R.S., Sale of Roxton Estate, 1-08-1851, Ref.X478/18-X478/61 and X478/19,

10. Huntingdon Archive Service., St. Neots U.R.C., St. Neots Old Meeting Church archive ref. FR16/8/2,

11. *ibid*. FR16/8/1

The Early Church

Dissent in Bedfordshire

John Brown BA, DD, in the first part of *The History of the Bedford Union of Christians*, published in 1896, speaks of the laxness in the established church that he suggests had led to the need for a great evangelical revival. He quotes the then Bishop of Liverpool, who had spoken about an Anglican clergy who, in the early part of the 18th century, were 'sunk in worldliness.... and within their own parishes... did as little and preached as seldom as possible'. [1]

That is not to suggest that the clergy at Roxton and Great Barford were as ineffective as the Bishop suggests. However, Roxton and Great Barford had been a united benefice since 1735, the latter village having the more suitable vicarage. By 1717 the Curate was admitting, 'I reside upon my cure, (ie. in Roxton village) but not in my vicarage house, it being very small and not capable of receiving my family'. The house at Roxton was completely inadequate and it is probable that subsequent vicars may have chosen to reside in Gt. Barford.[2] (A cottage that had been occupied by the churchwarden is known to have been situated to the front of the present churchyard. It was demolished about one hundred years ago). Perhaps the absence of a permanent clergy in Roxton Parish may have caused some problems; certainly by 1861 we read that a journey had to be made to Gt. Barford over the matter of a funeral. Gt. Barford may have seemed quite a distance to walk if parishioners wanted to see the vicar in times of difficulty, and there were many such times for the rural poor.

Countrywide such problems existed; there were also many communities, hamlets, farms and isolated dwellings that lay in the outer reaches of a parish that were almost never served by the Church. It was suggested by leading dissenting ministers who met in 1796 that 'in many parts of the County of Bedford there were people living at such distances from where the gospel was preached that they were never likely to hear it'. [3] A half-century earlier, many of these people had often walked many miles to crowd under a tree on a village green, to hear Wesley or an itinerant preacher; simple people flocked to Everton and the surrounding villages where the charismatic John Berridge preached, or to Colmworth and Bedford to hear the evangelist Timothy Matthews. These men all followed in the steps of the earlier John Bunyan. The time had come to think of centres and buildings where the gospel could be preached. Barns had been used where they were large enough and Wesley, in his journals related the story of how arriving in Bedford to preach one day in November 1759, he found the meeting was to be held in a loft above a barn where pigs were housed. The stench was so great that he wondered, 'Was ever a preaching place over a hog-sty before?' He went on, 'Surely, they love the Gospel who come to hear it in such a place. [4]

It was, suggested Brown, time for a revival and it was the leaders of the newly established Union that were to give Charles James Metcalfe, Gent., of Roxton, the support and encouragement to build his church.

The Bedfordshire Union of Christians

In worship and at Union meetings, Metcalfe met with the leaders of the Bedford Union. These men like Rev. Samuel Hillyard, of the First Church Bedford, as Bunyan Meeting was then known, had assembled at a meeting at Ampthill in 1796 out of which the Union was born. In October the following year an inaugural service was held. The Rev. Samuel Greethead preached the sermon that morning and it may have been through this mutual acquaintance, and his dealings with the leaders of the dissenting Christians in the locality, that Charles Metcalfe would almost certainly have met Sir Egerton Leigh. Sir Egerton was known to Greethead; the men had met at the founding of the London Missionary Society in 1795 when Sir Egerton chaired the inaugural meeting. Brown described Sir Egerton as, 'a godly baronet from Warwickshire'.[5] Sir Egerton had converted a farmhouse for worship on his estate at Little Harborough, near Rugby and would have been just the right person to encourage Charles with his plans for a meeting house at Roxton. Like Sir Egerton, Charles Metcalfe had been generous in his financial support of the *Bedford Union of Christians* since its inception. These men of reasonable substance shared Christian ideals and would most probably have talked of their plans. Only when there were places where the gospel could be preached, would it be possible to reach the masses of working labourers and their families in the rural areas.

There was opposition from the established church to the setting up of non-conformist places of worship, and Sir Egerton's building had been attacked and torn down even as it was being built; 'what the workmen put up in the day was by his enemies pulled down at night' so that guards were needed until the roof was on. [6] It was against this background that Charles and Elizabeth determined to follow their Christian convictions and looking at the lovely building that is their legacy, we might also say, their dreams, to build their chapel at Roxton.

Brown says that 'through the Bedfordshire Union religious zeal was stirred up countywide', but the meetings and plans for chapels were met by opposition and hostility. The Anglican Bishop Horley spoke of the growing movement of dissenting preaching as being led by, 'the enemy', and ridiculed the ordinary people who 'though having little education, were moved to preach the Christian gospel in the villages. However there was no doubt that it was towards the educated men who led the movement, that his vitriolic attack was directed. [7]

This, therefore, was the background of the time, as the newly-wed Charles and Elizabeth looked out of the front window of their home and contemplated where they would build their church. Across the little road that led from the centre of the village to the Bedford road, they could see an old thatched barn on the perimeter of their parkland. It lay in a slight dip in the land, behind thatched cottages on the village street. The barn was hired to William Brown, a Christian friend. It must have seemed the ideal spot and there was a ready-made building that they could convert.

Plans for a Meeting House at Roxton

Deciding on how best to convert the old barn for its new function may not have presented too much of a problem, since an appropriate style was already suggested by the building itself. Its position was such that it blended into the parkland and it would not have lent itself to drastic alterations in style. Hence there were no plans to build in the bold manner of other early nineteenth century Meeting Houses, where brick and stone were the favoured materials both in towns and villages.

There had been a fashion amongst the wealthy for developing ornate cottages as features in their pleasure parks since the mid 17th century. These buildings were thatched and were traditional in structure with much rustic bark-clad timberwork, simply, yet prettily fashioned. Altogether they were to seem part of an idyllic landscape, not as residences but as romantic retreats that offered escape from the responsibilities of everyday life. The architectural style was referred to as *Cottages Ornee*.

Charles and Elizabeth's plans began to take shape, and soon the work began to convert the old barn. There were skilled labourers employed on the estate that could do most of the work: a timber yard and plenty of rustic timber available in the woodland plantations. The workmen were adept at repairing the Estate cottages and skilled thatchers were available locally. As to how the design for the conversion was conceived we can only guess; Charles was able to travel about and would have seen a variety of such buildings in the parklands of wealthy acquaintances where *Cottage Ornee* gatehouses, retreats, or garden rooms were to be found. He may have engaged help to plan the conversion, that was surely founded in an extremely creative imagination to which the resultant beautiful building, in Regency Gothic Revival style, bears witness.

Transforming the Old Barn

The project must have caused a great deal of interest in the little community especially since many of the estate employees would have been working on the building. We can only speculate how long it took to transform the humble barn, with its low pitched roof, into the building which was illustrated by Mrs Metcalfe.

Chapel in Roxton Park; an engraving by Storey from a drawing by Mrs Metcalfe. BLARS Z63/21. A postcard depicting the image of Roxton Chapel attributed to Mrs. Metcalfe is featured on the back cover. Published c 1900. Gibbs collection.

The three bay barn was to have a door facing the village street, many ogee (arched gothic style) windows, three each on both the north and south sides, a thatched bell turret above the thatched roof and rustic bark-clad timber columns all round, importantly to support the protruding roof on the Eastern and Western ends. Inside, the earth floor was laid with bricks and the simple interior enlarged with a balcony to the eastern end that occupied one bay of the old building. This was supported by two iron columns. The walls were of traditional cottage material, wattle laths compacted with a clay/horsehair mix, known as daub. It was usual in this locality to dig clay for building as near to the work as possible. Where the lawn now dips to the southern side of the garden there was a pond which was not filled in until about nineteen sixty. This was most likely the source of the clay.

The interior walls were plastered with a traditional lime mix so that original beams were covered and a high ceiling formed. The interior was bright with light from the ten windows all around and the furniture would have been simple in keeping with the rustic building. It is likely that the benches in the body of the chapel are original, as are some very old forms now housed in the vestry and schoolroom. The early singing would have been unaccompanied - the harmonium was not invented until 1840. (The harmonium now in the vestry, accompanied the praises in the church from later in the nineteenth century when these instruments came into popular use in chapels and homes.)

The earliest known image of the church is a drawing that featured in the flyleaf of a book of hymns printed in London in 1825. It is attributed to Mrs Metcalfe, and either depicts the building before it was completed, and was an imagined drawing upon which the conversion was based, or it is a romantic interpretation of the finished church with idealised grounds showing pretty garden features with shrubs and trellis fencing, which seems to form the perimeter of the grounds. The pond is obviously in the foreground within the park.

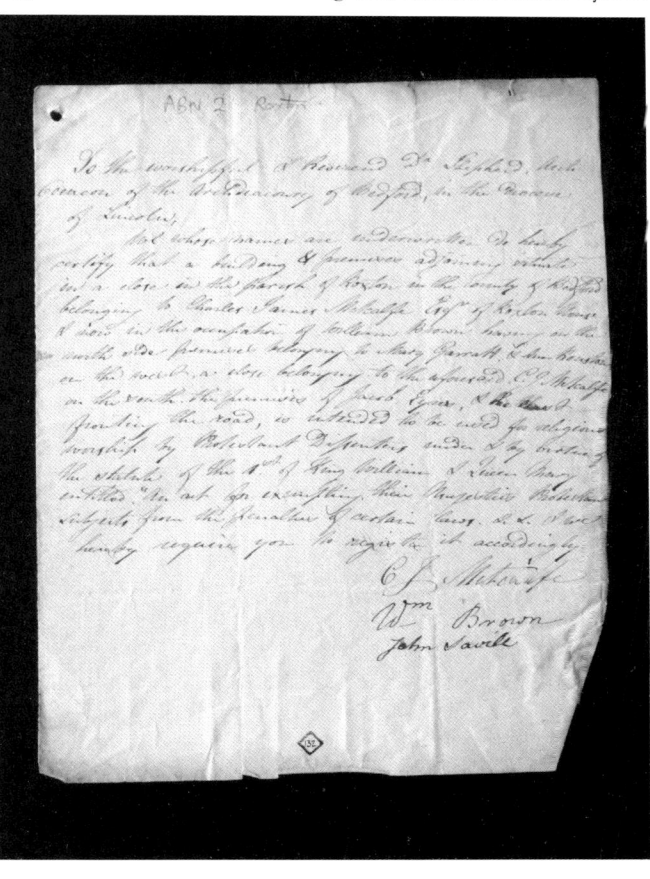

The application for a licence to hold religious worship at Roxton Barn. B.L.A.R.S.refs. ABN1/1; ABN2/132

Application is made for a Licence

The project, which was paid for entirely by Charles Metcalfe, may have taken quite a time to complete. However it was necessary to apply for a licence to hold religious worship in the new Chapel and an application was sent to Dr. Shepherd, Archdeacon of the Diocese of Bedford.[8] It read:

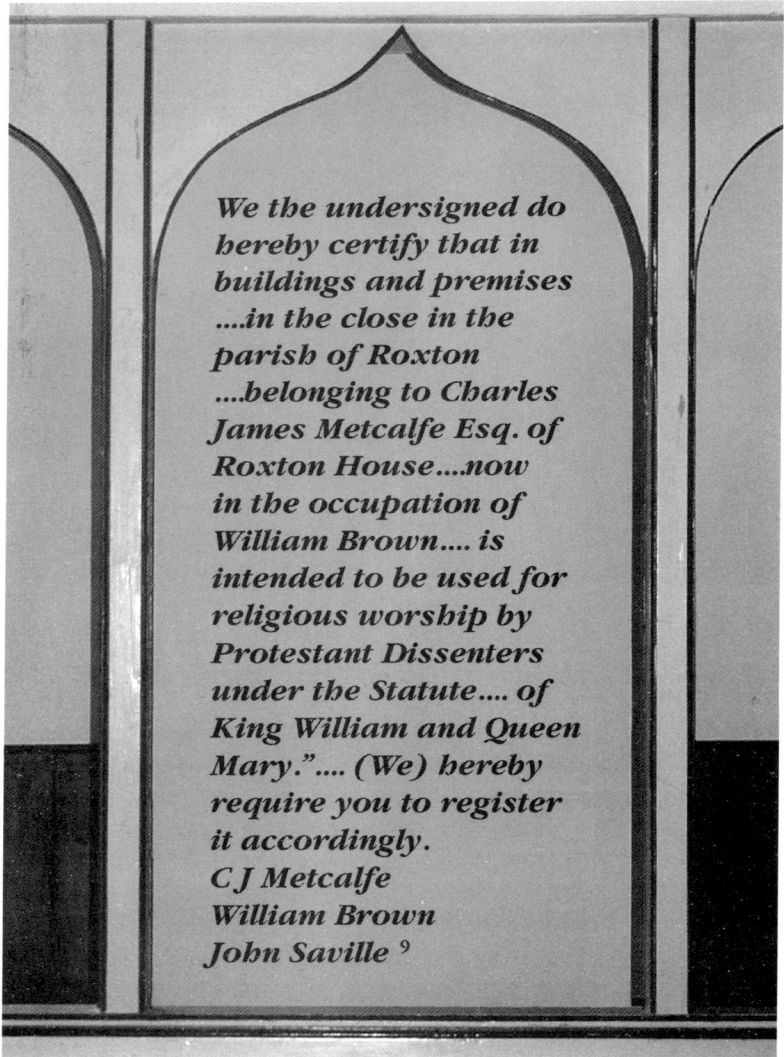

*We the undersigned do hereby certify that in buildings and premises ....in the close in the parish of Roxton ....belonging to Charles James Metcalfe Esq. of Roxton House....now in the occupation of William Brown.... is intended to be used for religious worship by Protestant Dissenters under the Statute.... of King William and Queen Mary.".... (We) hereby require you to register it accordingly.
CJ Metcalfe
William Brown
John Saville* [9]

Photograph of internal ogee arch   S. Eldridge

The First Service

The first Church Book, a small, green vellum bound, and evidently much handled record of the affairs of the early church records, on the opening pages, the events of May 31st 1808:

> On May 31st 1808 a barn belonging to C J Metcalfe was opened for occasional preaching on The Lord's Day and other evenings by ministers of different denominations.

It goes on to describe the first service that morning of the 8th May 1808, at which Rev. W. Stevens of Prescott Street, London preached. His text taken from 2 Timothy, 'but the word of God is not bound,' might well have referred to the freedom that these Christians had just won to preach the Gospel as they chose in their own meeting house. In the evening the Rev. S. Hillyard of Bedford preached; his sermon, based on a text taken from the book of Chronicles, 'Who then is willing to consecrate his service this day to the Lord?' must have challenged all who heard it. Dr Brown speaking some years later of Rev. Hillyard tells that, after many years of guiding the non-conformist movement forward, he became known affectionately as *'the Non-Conformist Bishop of Bedford'*.[10]

The Church records continue that since 'there were difficulties in obtaining supplies, (a preacher) every Sabbath evening, Mr M. (Metcalfe) conducted the services when no minister could be procured.' At this time and for a good number of years the family and a number of others from Roxton continued as members of the St. Neots Meeting.

Roxton Brethren take their leave of the St. Neots Old Meeting Fellows

There is then a jump in time in the Roxton records to 1821. At the same time the St. Neots church book records of their long-term minister, Charles Metcalfe's brother-in-law, 'The ministry of Mr. Morell ended in the year 1821, he having presided over the people nearly nineteen years. During this period the church and congregation greatly increased. Mr. Morell removed to the Accademical Institution at Wymondley. (Wymondley is recognised as having been one of the foremost training academies for Congregational ministers at that time). It was the usual practise that members wishing to transfer to another church notified their present church of their intentions and they were then formally dismissed from membership. Rev. Morell formally resigned his membership in 1822. In the same year on August 22nd we learn from the St. Neots church records that several members of the Metcalfe family, Elizabeth Bambridge,

Mr & Mrs Stearn, Susan Housden and one other Bainbridge (possibly James) were dismissed, to take up membership at (the new) church at Roxton. The records at Roxton state 'finding it very inconvenient to maintain their connection with the Church of Christ at St. Neots,' they 'felt it their duty to inform that Society,' of their intention to leave, 'and to adopt means of supporting the more constant opportunities for religious worship at Roxton, the attendance being equal to their expectations.' It seems that the occasional services were well supported and this was sufficient encouragement for the leaders at Roxton to formally establish their own church.

The First Members Establish the Church at Roxton

The Roxton Church Book indicates the enormity of the step that these few people were taking to leave an established church and branch out on their own; 'a few of us have .....considered forming a church at this place...to obviate the necessity of taking up so much of the Sabbath......by travelling to those places of worship with which we are connected.' The Church they prayed for was, we realise, not the building, for that was already there, but the people who would form the new Roxton Fellowship.

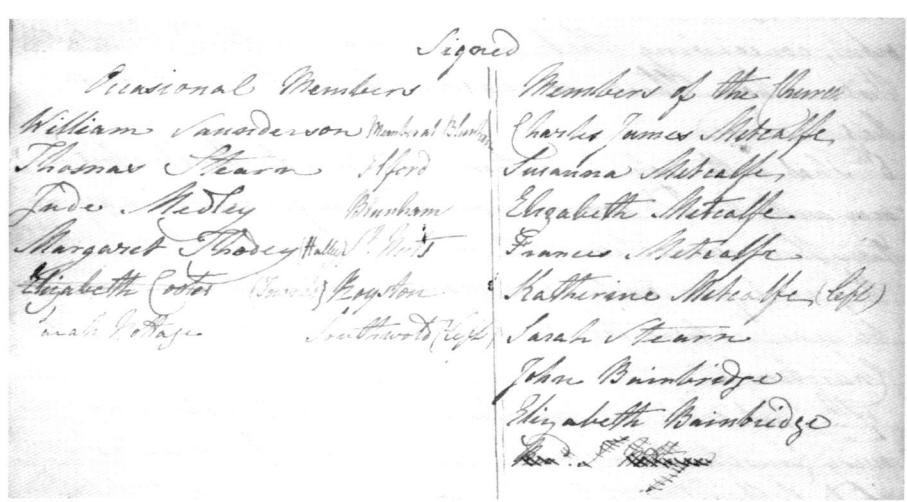

Signatures to the Resolutions adopted on the formation of the new Meeting House at Roxton.

Assembling in their new Meeting House they prayed and then agreed 'to unite as a church under the Great Shepherd of the Sheep; to walk together in love and Christian fellowship...his Blessing they trust and seek and (rely) on His wisdom and grace to direct them, and those they hope may be united to them.' They set their names to this testimony. In so doing they expressed the fervent trust that, 'Divine Providence should direct them to a settled pastor'. It stands as a record of the true faith and trust of this small group of people.

We know that at that time Charles Metcalfe referred to his new meeting house as *Roxton Barn*, from records of early donations that were sent to the London Missionary Society. [11]

On 31st July 1822 a series of nine formal resolutions that were to guide the formation and development of their Church were adopted and signed by fifteen persons, members and occasional members. In summary they were as follows:

> *1/ To form a Christian Society and henceforth to walk together as long as circumstances permit.*
>
> *2/ To watch over each other and to promote the spread of the gospel, both at home and abroad.*
>
> *3/ That the Society acknowledge no ecclesiastical authority other than the Scriptural model.*
>
> *4/ Admission to membership be open to anyone who demonstrates a personal Religion.*
>
> *5/ Any person, no matter what church they belong to, shall if they meet the above criteria, be welcomed with the Right hand of Fellowship into membership of this Society.*
>
> *6/ Any member of another church may temporarily join in communion if recommended through a testimonial from their own Pastor.*
>
> *7/ To join in fellowship with other Evangelical churches.*
>
> *8/ That a prospective member be recommended by a member and received only if approval is given by a majority.*
>
> *9/ That all members shall be pledged attend all meetings called at the church, especially The Lord's Supper, if circumstances permit.*

Within these resolutions the tenets of Congregationalism are enshrined; thereafter, although not referred to specifically in the Church Records, the Meeting House at Roxton was identified with the Congregational Movement.

The First Roxton Pastor

It was late in October of that year that the members agreed to invite Rev.Thomas Nottage of Southwold, Suffolk to preach to them. Initially he was invited for six months, and then was asked to become the first Pastor at the new Church. He agreed in a very florid letter dated November 1823, entreating his new congregation, 'most earnestly and affectionately to pray for him', praying that they would 'be filled with...all wisdom and understanding' and may 'approve things that are excellent ...and be sincere and without offence.'

He was welcomed to the pastorate at a special service at which the Rev's S. Hillyard minister at The Old Meeting, Bedford; T. Morell, theological tutor at Wymondley Accademy; Thomas Parker Bull, Tutor at the theological College at Newport Pagnell; I. Sloper, of Beccles and Rev. Holloway officiated and preached . Evening services followed and this must have completed a day in which the Christian hopes that Charles and Elizabeth Metcalfe had vested in their chapel, had been fulfilled. But the work of God had just begun in this place and it is due to their faith and vision that we have this beautiful building in which regular worship still takes place. The Service of the Lord's Supper was administered for the first time in July 1824 and the church book goes on to tell the story of the early church.

Membership Increases

During Rev. Nottage's ministry many new members joined the church; listed in the church book during those early years are members of the Cook, King, Wilkerson, Lightfoot, Hawkins and Barker families. With the new church securely established, it must have given Charles James Metcalfe especial delight when, on 24th September 1824, the members elected him to serve in office as their first Deacon. He was, as we shall see, to be the first of so many who were called to the Lord's work in this Church.

The first baptisms recorded in 1825, fittingly include that of Catherine Afflick, Charles and Elizabeth's daughter. Later, Sophia their daughter was baptised as well as children of the Bond, Lee, Hull, Kitely and Bainbridge families.

The book of "Roxton Hymns" is published.

In 1825 a little word book entitled Roxton Hymns was printed in London, most probably for use in the services; copies were also sold for a shilling. There was a tiny gold engraving on the otherwise plain front cover which showed the original chapel building and inside, the only illustration on the title page was a

When Baptized	Child's Christian Name & Sex	In what Parish born	When born	Parents' Names [so far as the same can be first Known of the Parties]	Abode	Parents' Profession	Sponsors of Parish B	[illegible]
1824 Nov. 7th	William Male	Roxton	August 8 1824	[illegible]	Roxton	Gentleman	Samuel Jones Susan Jones	Revd Ackley
1825 July 24th	Catharine Affleck Female	Roxton	Nov. 7 15th 1825	[illegible]	Roxton	Gentleman	[illegible]	Revd Ackley
1826 August 14th	John Male	Roxton	June 2nd 1826	[illegible]	Roxton	Gentleman	[illegible]	Revd Ackley
1827 July 1st	Anna Sophia Female	Roxton	May 14th 1827	[illegible]	Roxton	Gentleman	[illegible]	Revd Ackley
1828 Nov. 1st	Susan Female	Roxton	September 4th 1828	[illegible]	Roxton at the instance of Sponsors	Gentleman	[illegible]	Revd Ackley
1829 July 19th	Fanny Female	Roxton	February 1st 1829	[illegible]	Roxton	Gentleman	[illegible]	Revd Ackley

Baptism book and the first Baptisms recorded at the Roxton Church.

printed engraving based on a line drawing which was attributed to Mrs Metcalfe. It is a highly romanticised image of the rustic styled building, set within pretty grounds against the backdrop of trees.

Engraving of Roxton Barn Chapel as it looked in 1808; from the book of Roxton Hymns published c. 1825. Original drawing attributed to Mrs. Metcalfe. Ref. B.L.A.R.S. Z63/20

Postcards were also printed at some later date which featured this early illustration. It has been suggested that Rev. Thomas Morell, Charles James's brother-in-law, who is known to have written hymns could have been the author, however the book seems to have been attributed to an unidentified author of another work called 'An Old Year's Gift'. Although two copies were known to be kept in the chapel some fifty years ago, they have disappeared and no copy can be located today. The last known copy as indicated from the author's 1980's notes was inscribed; "A Reward from C.J.Metcalfe to Eliz..........ley 1827". *(We would very much like to find a copy – can you help?)*

The building is enlarged

It was either at this time or soon afterwards that the building was dramatically enlarged, to become the building that we know today. Whether this transformation took place during the eight years of Rev. Nottage's ministry we cannot be sure. Obviously Charles Metcalfe considered that enlargement and further improvements were necessary now that the fledgling church community was growing; provision outside the body of the church for meetings would reserve that original space specifically for worship.

It was now desirable that rooms be provided for prayer meetings and bible study; a schoolroom where village children would be taught both at Sunday School but also at a day school where instruction in basic skills like reading could take place. (Independents believed that helping the working classes towards self-improvement would inevitably lead to enhanced opportunities in their lives.)

South Porch – this entrance led via the vestry to the Metcalfe pew

Steve Eldridge

The additional space was built onto the old barn as wings or transepts at either side projecting to the South and North, abutting the bay at the western end of the building. These wings were in keeping with the original design, having elliptical ends so that within the rounded outer space small rooms were devised. There was provision of a study for the minister, as well as storage space in cupboards and tiny rooms, and toilets, (the old fashioned variety!). Raised pews were to be an added feature, including one for his family on the Southern side across the central bay. The space now provided for many more people: when large congregations that formerly would have overfilled the building now crowded to hear a preacher, partitions could be removed so that the side rooms opened up additional space into the main body of the building. Huge congregations by today's standards of easily 250 could be seated. This additional space has been used in recent times for large weddings.

A stained glass window adorned the study which is still furnished with the original rustic timber furniture.

To the South elevation, facing the Metcalfe's home, and designed to give direct entry from the park, a central porch entrance was created. Approached by rustic log steps the porch interior was finished in a style in keeping with the building, having a floor made of rustic tiles laid in a simple diagonal design and walls with panelling that was reminiscent of a grotto. Rough timberwork panels framed the entrance, and the walls and ceiling were panelled with fine chevron timberwork which finished with fir-cone ceiling bosses. The porch remains virtually the same to this day.

Thatched turrets were set midway on the roof ridge of each wing and large windows to the east and west let in spectacular light. The altered building could hardly have differed more from any other meeting house of its period; the beautiful building that resulted, and the one that we know today must be unique in its design. That its conception was inspirational and entirely appropriate to its function can only be truly understood when it is realised that the canopied roof and wings reveal a cruciform plan.

All these alterations funded by Mr. Metcalfe transformed the building into a practical church where worship and Christian and educational meetings could comfortably take place. Furthermore it afforded space for Christian based community social meetings and activities.

Until this time the main approach would have been from the Park entrance and the South, but it was necessary to create access direct from the main village street.

The Tiny Minister's Study in the Southern Transept : Steve Eldridge

Judging by the narrowness of the present day gateway it seems that a narrow piece of land was trimmed from the adjacent cottage garden, an estate property owned by Mr. Metcalfe, to forge an entrance pathway. Later pictures show how trees and a hedge crowded this route and only in the late 19th century was a small addition made to the land for a better positioning of the notice board.

An Early Crisis

It must have been with utter shock that the church leaders, attending a special meeting called on a Wednesday in July 1831, learned of the untimely resignation of their Pastor. It seemed that he had failed to adhere to his own strict rules of Christian behaviour and doubtless the words he had addressed to his prospective congregation just a few years earlier might now have been ringing in his ears! At a meeting of the members their deacon urged, 'Let all your things be done with charity' before they judged him. Today we cannot know what had caused Rev. Nottage's sudden fall from Grace, only that in his letter of resignation sent to Mr. Metcalfe, Rev. Nottage referred to a Mr. May as the person who he had offended. His conduct, he admitted to Mr. Metcalfe, though not of criminality, had nevertheless brought dishonour and scandal upon his office. In an earlier correspondence he had expressed his gratefulness to Mr. Metcalfe who no doubt provided accommodation and settled his salary. He ended his ministry at Roxton begging the prayers of the church. Rev. Nottage had held a position of respect within the local Independent Christian community, and had been invited to preach at Bedford at the Anniversary services of the Bedford Union of Christians in 1825, as well as at an important meeting in 1828.

What a scandal this would have been, and what gossip would have spread about the village! Members met in church and were addressed, most likely by Charles Metcalfe. They were urged to deplore the discredit brought upon the cause of religion and the, 'evil speaking...lying and un-charitableness (of which many among you know more than myself)'. (He was suggesting that the members would have heard more than he had since they mixed freely with other ordinary villagers). The meeting ended with a resolve to pray for their discredited Pastor 'and our own peculiar situation'.

Local ministers came to the aid of the church, conducting services until arrangements were made for the Rev. H. Winzar to preach during September and October 1835. He began his pastorate in 1835.

Notes

1. John Brown B.A.D.D., *Centenary Celebrations of the Bedfordshire Union of Christians*. The Congregational Union of England and Wales 1896, p.9-10

2. Patricia Bell (ed.) *Episcopal Visitations in Bedfordshire 1706-1720*, Bedfordshire Historical Record Society, Vol. 81, 2002, p. 161.

3. John Brown B.A.D.D., *ibid*, p.17. There follows a proposal to set up 'a spiritual, cordial and active union of all real Christians.'

4. G. M. Seward quotes *The Journals of John Wesley* in *John Wesley in Bedfordshire*, Bedfordshire Magazine, Vol.3, No. 18 Autumn 1951. p.60.

5. John Brown B.A.D.D., *ibid*, p.25.

6. *ibid*, p.25

7. *ibid*, Brown quotes Bishop Horley, 'The pastor is often, in appearance at least, an illiterate peasant or mechanic....the congregation is visited occasionally by preachers....and Sunday schools are opened....(which)....if we may judge from appearances, their own means would be altogether inadequate (to support.)'. p.39-40

8. BLARS ref. ABN1 and 2

9. H.G.Tibbutt, *Roxton Congregational Church 1808-1958* pub. Roxton Congregational Church May 1958, p.6

10. John Brown B.A.D.D., *ibid*, p.74.

11. H.G.Tibbutt. Roxton Congregational Church 1808-1958. P.6.

Rev. John Brown, B.A., D.D., biographical note:

Rev. John Brown B.A., D.D., of Bedford was author of 'The History of the Bedford Union of Christians', published in 1896. It documented the founding of the Union by Rev. Samuel Greethead and told of the first one hundred years and of the support given to the village churches during that time. He served as president of the Union for twenty-four years from 1879-1903 and as Pastor of Bunyan Meeting , Bedford for almost forty years until 1903. He was an acclaimed historian who wrote amongst other works, the history of John Bunyan and is acknowledged by Rev. D. prothero, B.A., B. Sc., B.D., in 'Part 11: the Story of the Union Continued, 1897-1946', to have 'brought much honour upon the Union by his literary work and by his appiontment to the chair of the Congregational Union in 1891'. He was further called to address the students of Divinity at Yale in 1899. He was held in high esteem throughout the county of Bedford and ministry at Bedford and to the country churches was acclaimed and long remembered.

A Period of Growth 1835-1851

It is apparent from the records that Rev. Winzar must have been a man of action; 'I deem it a privilege to come amongst an affectionate and united people,' he wrote,

'I intend....to be with you in the course of the next week.' His records in the Church book, in contrast to those of the prosaic Rev. Nottage, were short and to the point. We learn nothing of texts, earnest admonitions and fervent prayers, but have a record of steady growth in the membership, baptism into the Church and a consolidation of the Christian ideals that had already been established. The Rev. Winzar was publically recognised as pastor of Roxton Independent Meeting at a special service on April 24th 1832.

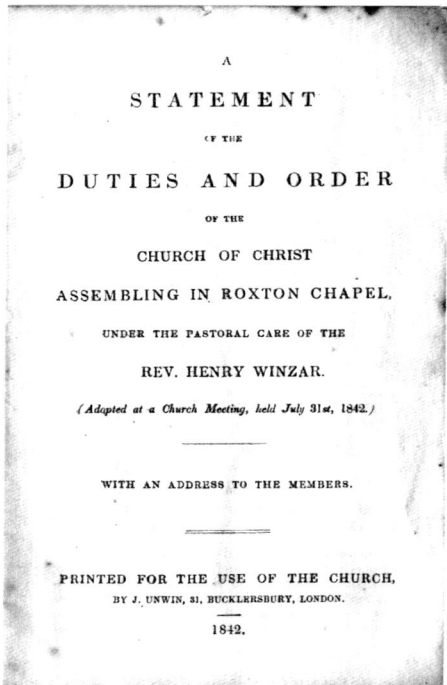

The book of Regulations for the Government of the Independent Dissenting Church at Roxton published 1842. Roxton Chapel

Officiating at his ordination were eminent teachers from both Highbury and Wymondley colleges and once again, Rev. S. Hillyard from Bedford.

The new Pastor obviously set to work immediately and drew up a list of eighteen regulations for his Church members. Written in the Church Book they were to be printed in a booklet in 1842.

Determined to set absolute Godly standards for his flock these extensive rules were for their guidance and spelled out the standards of behaviour expected of all members of the fellowship: eventually each member would have a copy. Too lengthy to reproduce here they generally elaborated on the earlier rules but add some others that members are expected to adhere to. Rule four specifies, 'No person who attends public dances, theatres, or card tables (and frequents) public houses unnecessarily, or who travels on The Lord's Day for business or pleasure can be received a member of this church.' Neither were they to 'bear tales' or 'gamble'. Rule seventeen states, 'No member is to contract marriage with an irreligious person' unless the marriage contract had been made previously - in which case, 'the regulation cannot be enforced'.

Most of the rules are less controversial and simply spell out the central tenets enshrined in Congregationalism, a denomination that had begun as early as 1640 when the Independent and Congregational church had been founded. This Independent movement 'developed after the post-Reformation ejection of non-conforming ministers from the Church of England'.[1] Pre-eminent to Congregationalism is the practice that all members take an equal part in deciding on any matter pertaining to the organisation and running of their church Decision making is not vested in any leader or imposed by any authority set above the membership of the individual church Meeting.

Once membership had been sanctioned by the majority, regular attendance at worship and at the Lord's Table was then almost unconditional. Members who did not comply were admonished and sanctioned by dismissal from membership, whether temporary or at times permanent.

On August 11th 1837 the Congregational church at Roxton was registered for marriages. It was listed as the third church in the Bedford Register No. 375, after Bunyan Meeting and Howard Congregational.

Growth of Membership and Baptism at Roxton Meeting

Church membership increased year on year throughout Rev. Winzar's ministry. Several members of the Metcalfe family were admitted to membership, including Elizabeth his wife, and his son. Members came from Chawston, Colesden, Wyboston, Little End (Eaton Socon), Gt. Barford, and from as far afield as St. Neots and Bolnhurst. There is early mention of families that were to be associated with the church over many years; we find Bambridge (sp. Bainbridge) with a note stating 'at the formation of the church'; King, Livett (sp. Levett), Darrington, Jefferies (sp. Jeffries), Gilbert and Jarvis.

There were also prominent local families like the Ayers', farmers from Colesden and the Wilkerson's of Chawston.

Members who moved to the locality transferred from previous churches and John Newling who came from Melbourne, Hertfordshire became a valued member of the church, deacon and occasional preacher. By the mid 1840's the membership numbered more than one hundred. It had been the custom that new members should be welcomed into membership by a handshake offered by each existing member. Unsurprisingly people found this rather wearisome! The practice was modified and even today the *Right hand of Fellowship* as it is known, is given by the Pastor and Deacons only. Many of these early members had received no education and alongside their name entered in the Church Register by the Pastor, they put their mark as a cross.

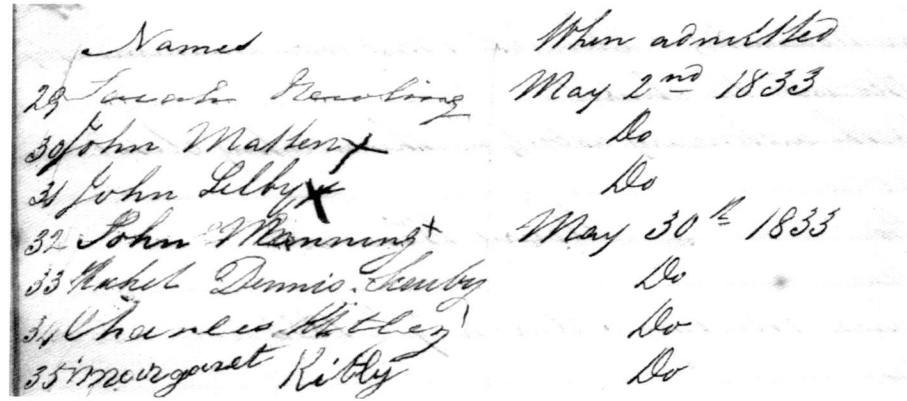

Examples of early members who could not write their names. Register of Members.

There were many baptisms during these years and multiple baptisms often occurred. On January 5th 1834, four children of the Lee family ranging from 4 months to 9 years, and also adults William Payne and James Barker Bond were baptised. That same year, three days of baptism were held on July 23rd, 25th and 26th when a total of thirteen members of the Beale, Hull, Kitely, Haines, Holden, Wilkerson, Harpur and Pratt families were baptised. Much useful information for today's family historians can be obtained from the early registers. eg. The entry in 1833, when Betsy, daughter of Jerry Lee a shoemaker and his wife, Sophia, nee Franklin, was baptised.

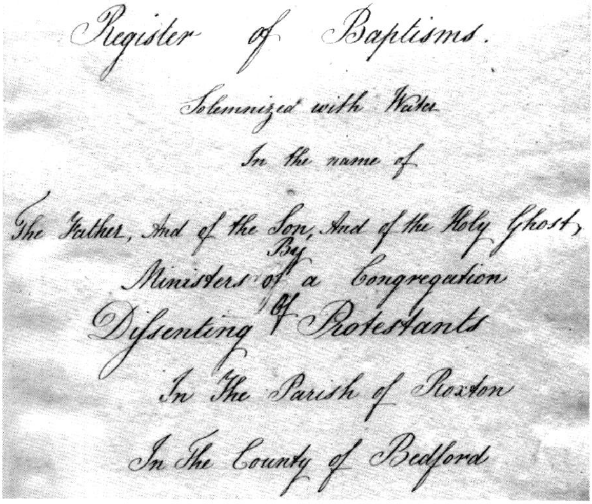

Register of Baptisms.

Solemnized with Water

In the name of

The Father, And of the Son, And of the Holy Ghost, By Ministers of a Congregation of Dissenting Protestants

In The Parish of Roxton

In The County of Bedford

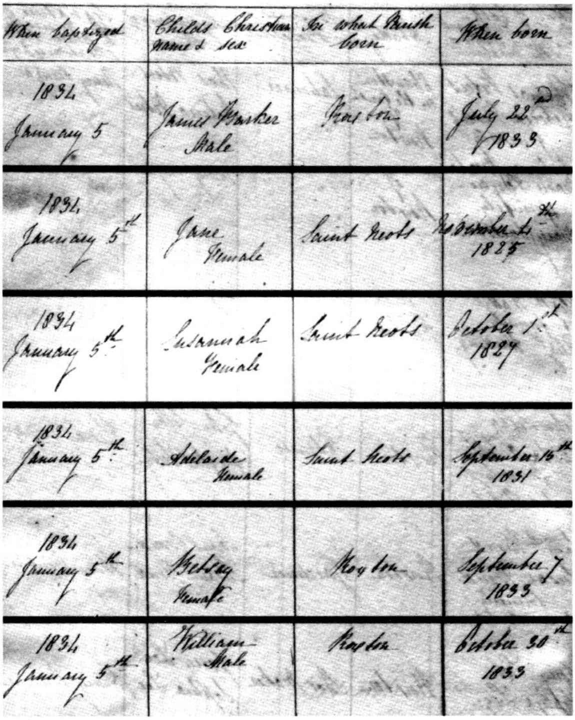

When baptized	Child's Christian name & sex	In what Parish born	When born
1834 January 5	James Barker Male	Roxton	July 22nd 1833
1834 January 5th	Jane Female	Saint Neots	November 1st 1825
1834 January 5th	Susannah Female	Saint Neots	October 1st 1827
1834 January 5th	Adelaide Female	Saint Neots	September 14th 1831
1834 January 5th	Betsy Female	Roxton	September 7 1833
1834 January 5th	William Male	Roxton	October 30th 1833

Top: Baptism Register.
Bottom: A Multiple Baptism in 1854 — often all the children of a family were baptised at the same time. Roxton Baptism Book

The rule that seems to have given the biggest problem was to keep up attendance at The Lord's Supper. Richard Lee found this a problem in 1840 and was excluded for 'inconsistency', but there were many other reasons for dismissal from membership during the mid-eighteenth century when behaviour fell below the expected standard. In 1847 there were two alehouses in the village, *The Chequers and The Royal Oak. (The Pear Tree beer-house was built shortly afterwards in 1851).* That year Samuel Bond was suspended for six months, 'for want of sobriety'. Temptation to drink was obviously his downfall despite the fact that he was a valued Church member who had once been appointed to visit and talk with prospective members, as was the practice. Richard Lee was also dismissed for 'want of honesty in discharging his debts and frequenting public houses'. Two women were also suspended for debts that they ran up and made no attempt to settle. In 1840 another two women were suspended for 'the sin of un-chastity'. In 1835 John Manning was charged with 'immorality'. He admitted his fault and the reports against him being established 'as falsehoods', he was suspended from The Lord's Supper once only. The Pastor took this opportunity to warn others against taking drink in public houses. Drink seems to have been a temptation for one or two of these labourers!

Protestors in the Chapel!

When Samuel Bond and John Manning failed to attend "the Ordinances", (what we now call Holy Communion) they must have expected to be judged harshly. It followed that they were suspended - but only temporarily. Thereafter the two decided on *protest action* to show how they felt about such harsh judgement and in 1839 we read, 'Samuel Bond and John Manning..... were suspended in 1834 and 1835 for a short while each, but thought it right to decline sitting down (during) The Lord's Supper ever since'!

Fresh Fields and Pastures New

When members moved away it was the practice that they asked to be dismissed from the church and to be recommended to a specific church in their new locality; letters were sent to and fro by the respective Pastors. In September 1834 founder members John and Elizabeth Bainbridge asked for dismissal as they were about to leave for America. This truly was a move into the unknown and the members unanimously commended them to the fellowship of whichever Church, 'as Providence may direct them'. Charles and Elizabeth Metcalfe must have mourned the departure of friends who had been alongside them worshipping at St.Neots and had supported them all through the building and establishment of the Fellowship at Roxton. Six months later a letter received from them, 'conveyed tidings of their comfort' which reassured their many friends at the church. Others too left for far off places in search of a new life. In 1834 Sarah and Margaret Kiteley left for Australia and the following year Mr. P. George emigrated to New Zealand. The loss of Jabez Hawkins when he moved to Wilden in 1848 would have been keenly felt since he had been a valued assistant preacher.

Charles James Metcalfe Esq. Sheriff of the County

During the 1830's Charles Metcalfe Esq. enjoyed a favourable position in public life. He had been nominated for the position of Sheriff of the County both in 1832 and 1833 and appointed to that position at a court in Brighton on February 7th 1835. The report of the proceedings in The London Gazette opens:

PRESENT

The King's Most Excellent Majesty in Council.
SHERIFFS appointed by His Majesty in Council for the Year.
Charles James Metcalfe, Bedfordshire

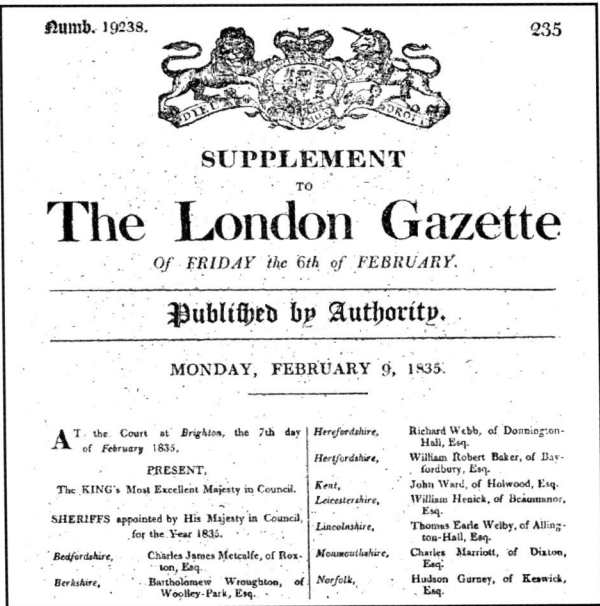

The official Notice from the London Gazette of Friday the 6th February, 1835.
London Gazette Website

Charles Metcalfe therefore had numerous responsibilities as the Sheriff of the County and no doubt he was absent from his home in pursuit of his public duties. However his Christian Faith was one of the most important things that governed his life and doubtless he found time among his other duties to carry on his work as a deacon, ever watchful that God's work was continuing under the exemplary leadership of Rev. Winzar. In 1834 a second deacon, John Newling, was appointed to help with the day-to-day running of church affairs. As membership increased so did the workload for the deacons who were now elected to serve for three years.

The Day to Day Life of the Church

In 1846 we find the first mention of tea being served, ' at five o'clock members sat down in the schoolroom for tea,' before the annual church meeting which had always been held in late December or early January. This was the start of a tradition of serving refreshments that continues today. We must remember that people travelled quite a distance, often on foot, or by horse-drawn buggy, so chapels established a tradition of offering simple refreshment before or after important business or worship meetings.

Lady members were appointed as sick visitors, often serving for many years. Several of the Metcalfe ladies undertook this work, along with many other ladies who are mentioned down the years.

There is an oral tradition that a converted Christian Princess of an American Indian tribe visited Roxton to speak at a Christian meeting at the chapel. She was said to have stayed as a guest of Charles and Elizabeth Metcalfe at Roxton House. (Marjorie Gosling told how the story had been recounted to her mother before her.)

The First School in the Village

A day school was held in the Chapel Schoolroom and as early as 1833 a report submitted to the National Society and The British and Foreign School Society confirmed that there was a Congregational Infant School attended by 27 children. It went on to add that a Congregational daily school had been started that year; 48 were being taught; 17 boys attended during the winter evenings. These schools were supported by donations as well as payments by parents [2] It is believed that the Misses Metcalfe, Charles's sisters devoted time to teaching children from the village. Mrs. Mary Buckle, a schoolmistress who lived in the village and was listed as a member may also have taught the children.

The room was light, warmed by a central coal stove and equipped with forms and drop down work-benches. This is also where a Sunday School would have been held. The 1833 report continues that there were two Sunday schools in the village, the Church of England taught 30 boys; the Congregational taught 42 boys and 80 girls. Episcopal returns (reports to the bishop) in 1846/7 stated that there was no British School in Roxton, despite the fact that in 1836 a grant of £50 had been made to provide such a school. The report went on to state that 'the people are miserably poor and there are no resident gentry.' [2] However Metcalfe family members are shown to be residing at Roxton House both on the 1841 and 1851 census's, although in 1851 Charles James and Elizabeth were unrecorded and were probably travelling at the time. (Metcalfe family anecdotal supposition is that Charles and Elizabeth muddled through and were not efficient at running the estate. This might well imply that they therefore took little account of the condition of the village people and yet there is convincing evidence to show that the people held them in high regard. The supposition is most likely based on evidence that loans were taken out periodically to furnish the expenses of their extended family).

Adult Improvement Classes

Adult Church members found time during the evenings for Bible studies, despite the working day being six am to six pm, with the men needing to tend gardens or allotments and look after life-stock on the estate farms. Recreational reading was also encouraged by Mrs Metcalfe who set up a lending library of suitable novels, some no doubt from her own bookshelves. This philanthropic enterprise which encouraged the development of reading skills was no doubt one of the things that endeared this lady to the community. The rules for the lending library were set out inside the book which states, 'provided by Mrs. Metcalfe and Daughters, with some assistance from *The Religious Tract Society.*' Mr. James Bond, librarian is stated here.

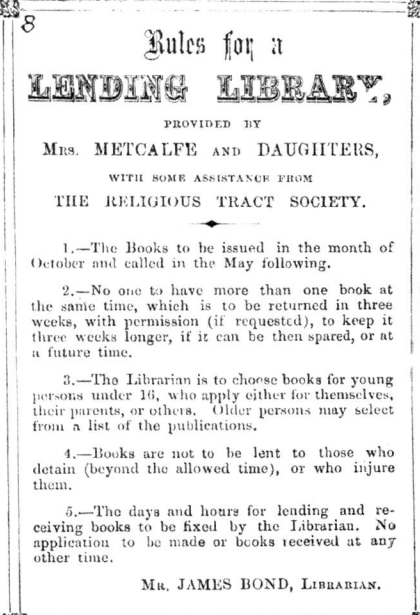

The Lending Library Rules inside a copy of 'Mrs. Elizabeth Fry – biographical Series no 31' Roxton Chapel

The Pattern of Worship.

The number attending services might well have swelled to two or three times the membership, especially in the summer months or when a special preacher was to give a sermon. Nevertheless in 1839 the Pastor expressed concern at the 'number of unconverted persons' in the neighbourhood. A revival of religion was proposed and a week of meetings planned. Services were held between six and seven in the mornings and again in the evenings. This revival was aimed, he said, at the 'ungodly inhabitants of the neighbouring villages' and we learn that many attended. We must remember that in the mid-nineteenth century the combined population of the nearby hamlets of Chawston and Colesden exceeded that of Roxton. Rev. Winzar clearly believed that there were many souls to harvest for The Lord. (In 1806 there had been 469 inhabitants of Roxton; this had grown considerably to 622 by 1851). [4] He would also have been concerned that the Latter Day Saints (Mormons) were making numerous converts in North Bedfordshire during the 1840's. His Roxton Church supported preachers who went to Wyboston, Wilden and a hamlet of Eaton Parish as well as to Colesden and Chawston. [5]

He was not without humour, albeit rather ironic in tone; after recording that he had administered The Lord's Supper at a meeting in 1846 he continued 'not without (*it is hoped*) the presence of The Great Master of the Feast'!

During his ministry an afternoon service was begun throughout the winter months. A practical move since the interior of the building depended on lamps to light it and travel was more difficult in the evening light. In the 20th century this practice was re-instated.

It was during this time that the Rev. Thomas Pierson Richardson visited the Anglican Church prior to taking up ministry here in 1847. He was to lead the Roxton and Gt. Barford congregations for twenty-eight years until 1875. His obituary in the Parish Magazine of 1894 relates his first visit to the village when he found, 'the church in very bad repair and the Parish distracted by the division caused by their principal landowner having forsaken the Church of England.' It cannot be denied that the Church of England here suffered a dearth of support both financial and in numbers of worshippers because Charles Metcalfe Esq. had broken away from the Anglican Church.

Portent of Change

At a meeting in April 1848 the Pastor referred to, 'some reasons rendering it desirable to appoint another deacon', but these reasons were not made clear in the minutes or possibly even to those members who were present. It could be assumed that Charles Metcalfe Esq., being extremely busy, was unable to devote sufficient time to his church duties. Consequently Rev. Winzar recommended Charles Metcalfe Jnr. to the post of third deacon, an appointment that was supported unanimously.

The Round Gatehouse is Built

According to the date marked on a brick at the back of the round gatehouse situated at the Western entrance to the park, this little house dates from 1848. Although similar in appearance to the chapel it has distinctly different windows, although in the gothic style. Since then it had been inhabited and families had been brought up there, until the 1960's when it was considered uninhabitable since it had no piped water or modern drainage.

The New Park Gatehouse- a brick in the south wall denotes its date as 1848.   *S. Gibbs*

Unexpected Resignations

Church business continued as usual during the next two years until most unusually, on Sunday May 20th 1850, an extraordinary meeting was called at which members were given confirmation that Charles Metcalfe Jnr. was about to leave Chawston (Manor) House for Guernsey. It may have been the first that members had heard of this imminent departure, but rumours were surely abroad in the neighbourhood. It was, we read, 'for their enhanced prosperity' that the family were to move.

Prayers were offered for the family and sympathy expressed with him and his family in what is described as 'the painful circumstances' which had brought about their separation from each other. The minutes convey a palpable sense of loss and sadness but do nothing to hint at the cause or magnitude of the families' problems. In August, Charles Metcalfe Jnr. requested dismissal from membership for himself, his wife Louisa and two servants, Henrietta Emery and one un-named, to a church in Guernsey. Louisa had carried out many pastoral duties for the church since becoming a member in 1845. She was pregnant with her second child when they departed for Guernsey.

The Founder Resigns

Charles Metcalfe Esq. tendered his resignation as senior deacon, in writing on September 1st 1850. His letter referred to 'weakness preventing him from fulfilling his duties'. This request at first met with rejection but that was merely to symbolise the respect and affection in which he, Mrs Metcalfe and their whole family were held. Members then expressed their 'deep sense of the invaluable services which he had been able to render during the 26 years of his holding (office)'. They went on to express their feeling of indebtedness to him, recorded as follows;

> *'In him under God they owe it that a place for the worship of the Most High God had been provided and maintained: in him has devolved a principal share in the support of the ministry of the gospel and the religious institution connected with the place: his talents have always been, when required, at the service of the Church in supplying the pulpit and conducting prayer meetings in the Pastor's absence; and in fulfilling the deacon's office he has been invariably kind and considerate alike to Pastor and people, always ready for every good word and work, walking always in the fear of God.*

Whether the members knew what had brought about this withdrawal from his beloved Chapel we cannot know but they must have realised that an event of cataclysmic proportions had occurred. What had actually befallen him would very soon have been the subject of rumour, supposition and exaggeration. In this instance however, it would hardly have been possible to exaggerate matters beyond the reality that was to emerge.

The Demise of the Metcalfe Family

Charles Metcalfe Jnr. so family history tells, along with William Leopold Metcalfe, had been persuaded by Charles May, one of his mother's brothers, to invest speculatively in the manufacture of soap at a premises in Gt. Yarmouth. This venture, whether ill-advised or just as a result of dreadful misfortune, had failed dramatically and as a result the shareholders were called upon to settle enormous debts

Charles Metcalfe Jnr. had probably been the mainstay of the estate, in charge of its day-to-day running while his elderly father led a somewhat quieter life. By 1850 he feared that bankruptcy loomed and he and his family had left his parents and Roxton in the hope of a better or was it a quieter life, in Guernsey? It would seem that although it was Charles Jnr. who had been persuaded to venture into the soap business, it had been Charles James Esq. who had been persuaded to stand surety for this venture.

A Petition for adjudication for Bankruptcy was filed against the three on 18th March 1851 and proceedings were begun in the Court of Bankruptcy against Charles May of Norwich, William Leopold Metcalfe of Gt. Yarmouth and Charles James Metcalfe of Roxton, Bedfordshire. The court charged the co-partners to attend at the court on 11th April and on 13th May, 'to make a full discovery of and disclosure of their estates and effects'. Their creditors were to, 'come prepared to prove their debts'. Of the three shareholders, it seems that it was Charles Metcalfe Esq. only who held assets that could be realised to settle the debts involved. The proceedings that dragged on in court are detailed in the London Gazette. It became clear that the family were in a serious financial position and Charles and Elizabeth must have been devastated. Their world was about to implode as they faced the reality of their situation. Charles was forced to sell the estate and although £68.250.00 was realised, apparently in addition to any prior claims that the court of Bankruptcy had on these assets the balance was needed to settle debts on the Roxton estate. [6]

Rev. Winzar Resigns

The Pastor's earnest prayers for Charles Metcalfe had been that 'grace and peace (would be) with his spirit to cheer his declining days', but he must have been concerned too for himself and his family. He had led a comfortable life supported and befriended by Charles Metcalfe Esq., and no doubt having the provision of a decent cottage for his wife, children and servants, but this was all to change.

At the annual Meeting of the members held in January 1851 Rev. Winzar resigned the pastorate at Roxton. He had presided over the church throughout nineteen years and evangelised for Christ's Kingdom from the pulpit in this place. A letter commending him to his new church spoke of his 'interest in the best welfare of the young' and the increased membership that told of his effective ministry adding with sad irony that Roxton Fellowship's "loss (which we feel deeply), is your gain'.

Rev. Winzar departed for his new pastorate to a Church at High Wycombe in the Spring of 1851.

Notes

1. Gerald T. Rimmington, *Congregationalism and Society in Leicester 1872-1914*, The Local Historian, Vol. 37, No. 1, p.29.

2. ibid.

3. ibid.

4. See www.bedfordhsire.gov.uk/archives/communityarchives/Roxton/introduction

5. H.G.Tibbutt. Roxton Congregational Church 1808-1958, Roxton Congregational Church ,p. 10 quoting from The Evangelical Magazine 1833, p.508.

6. Metcalfe papers and the wills of James Metcalfe and William Metcalfe are held by B.L.A.R.S.

Difficult Times 1851-1900

Changing Times and the Rural Poor.

People living in rural communities would have found life in the mid-nineteenth century difficult. With a rising population overcrowding was widespread and people lived in poorly repaired cottages with few facilities. The 1861 Census provides evidence that unusually, people in Roxton village were extremely self-sufficient, having trades people who could service all their needs within the community. This was somewhat unusual since at this time a migration of craftspeople had begun; this movement of people was to develop into a mass migration of agricultural labourers during the 1870's. The mid-eighteen hundreds were a time when poverty was endemic in rural villages, wages were low - due in part to a drop in corn prices - and women needed to work to help support the family. Income was supplemented by making lace or plaiting straw, skills which even the small children learned. Boys especially were paid for fieldwork, the school log during the 1870's reports children as absent for bird scaring, plant dropping, picking up potatoes, or minding horses by the roadside;[1] all tasks that paid extra into a families' meagre income. Families also relied on wheat gleaned at harvest-time either to be milled for making bread or to feed poultry. Hens were kept for laying and for the cook-pot. The elderly poor who could not work relied on the support of their families, and many extended families were crowded into small cottages. Without familial support they could find themselves sent to the workhouse for their final years – an ignominious fate, the fear of which lingered long in the consciousness of a generation that had witnessed or been told about it.

This was a time when women tended to marry when they were older, having first worked *in service* for several years and hence often married men who were several years their junior. These tended to be women of strong character and although it was to be almost one hundred years before any woman was to be elected to office in the Church, nevertheless more women than men took up membership in these early decades. They were used to hard work and brought up large families; members William and Betsy Bambridge raised ten children. Later in the nineteenth century younger men were attracted to new kinds of employment that took them away from their home villages, as the railway spread across the country. The promise of higher wages attracted many and led to a general boon; Rowland (Bainbridge) son of Wm. and Betsy Bambridge, with his wife Emma, ceased membership and left the village with his younger brother to work on the railway at Nottingham.

The new Lord of the Manor, Robert Delap, did not live in the village and so did not need the house in the parkland. In modern terms the purchase of the estate was merely an investment opportunity and he is remembered as being, 'disinterested and neglectful of the village'.[2] He allowed the Metcalfe family to live on there for the time being; probably sympathising with Charles Metcalfe Esq. in his demise.

A Leaderless Church

Members of the chapel at Roxton in 1851, no doubt reeling from the shock of losing their founder and supporter and then their Pastor, found themselves having to run their church unaided for the first time. There are no minutes for 1852 but their old Pastor, Henry Winzar was invited back, 'by the younger deacons' to preside at the annual meeting in 1853. He referred to the 'the great favour the Lord had bestowed upon the Church in keeping so many together during the trying circumstances in which it was placed.' The members would look to their deacons, John and Thomas Newling for guidance. The deacons would have been educated men who would have met with respect, and who could keep the church books written up. Sadly in August that year we read that 'John Newling, deacon for 25years departed this life'. For the first time in the history of the church Thomas Newling read a statement of church finances. Prior to his demise Charles Metcalfe Esq. had taken care of all such matters. Now the church needed to be self sufficient and the deacons would need to concentrate on the day-to-day running of the Church, and find preachers to serve the pulpit. John Manning was appointed deacon in 1860. The deacons proved to be less than efficient at keeping up the Church records, hence we know far less about the next forty years from the Church Book.

A difficult period ensued and by 1853 several members had left or failed to attend meetings, however two had rejoined on returning to the village and for the first time in the 45 year history of the Church mention is given of the reading of a statement of their financial affairs at a meeting. Another deacon was needed and Hugh Bentley appointed. It was time to take stock of the situation and a list of the members was drawn up in the Church book. Then in December arrangements were made for Mr. Jos. Williams a student from the Cotton End (Bedfordshire) Academy, to take over pastoral duties for six months. He was to stay in the village Friday to Monday. There followed similar arrangements with other students, who were supportive during these difficult times, but since these arrangements were of a temporary nature, a more permanent remedy was needed.

The situation at Roxton became more difficult as the Cotton End Academy moved towards closure. There and at the Bedford Academy at Bunyan Meeting, students had been trained for the Congregational and Missionary ministries. In the final years numbers of students declined, only five attending in 1866; this meant that few were available to help in the village churches. 'Mr. Brown (is) missing us very much for the Village Stations', wrote a former student who had heard of the closures.[3] These academies had been centres of higher Education, teaching not only divinity but the classical languages and had sent many educated men to mission posts abroad through The London Missionary Society.

Mr. Charles Metcalfe Jnr. had written in support of the deacons in March or April 1855 when they had applied to the Congregational Home Missionary Society for someone to minister to Roxton; probably concerning himself with this matter when he returned for his father's funeral. The request met with refusal and the church was kept going with the help of visiting preachers until 1860.

Death of the Founder of Roxton Chapel, 1855

It was in the February of 1855 that Charles James Metcalfe Esq. founder of the Independent Chapel at Roxton died. The Church book records his 'invaluable service to the Church in the cause of God'. He was laid to rest in the Parish churchyard in the family tomb. His life is recorded on a simple obelisk, much faded at this time, it states quite simply that he died on February 20th 1855 in his 69th year. On the bottom of the memorial is a simply worded affirmation that through his life he demonstrated that he truly believed: that it is *"Christ who is our Hope"*.[4]

The Metcalfe Memorial in Roxton Church Graveyard   *Stella Gibbs*

Members 'black' an Annual Meeting – Rev. J.W.Rolls appointed

When only three of the seventy members attended an important meeting called on January 30th 1860 Hugh Bentley and John Manning, deacons, knew something was wrong. They later learned that most members felt that the church *could* afford to pay a minister's salary. Jarred into immediate action the deacons sought advice and all agreed to invite Rev. J W Rolls, a former student at Cotton End, presently at Halifax, to the position. He recorded, 'Commenced my labours at Roxton, as Pastor of the Independent Church, April 1st 1860'. He stayed for over twelve years. His records are sparse – he admits that only those meetings at which someone was admitted (to membership) or when some particular business occurred are recorded. The meetings were held in the *Schoolroom;* the term first appears in the records in 1859 and continues to the present day. Membership increased during the ministry of Rev. Rolls swelling by a dozen between March and June of 1866. It must have cheered the older members to see their fellowship growing.

'A Case of Priestly Intolerance at Roxton', Bedfordshire Mercury Newspaper.

This was the newspaper headline reporting an incident that occurred in 1861. It seems that the Rector of the Parish Church, the Rev. Pierson Richardson refused to bury Charlotte the infant daughter of Wm. King, a member of the Independent Church because the child had not been baptised. This incident was reported in the Bedfordshire Mercury alongside a letter that made scathing comment under the title, *The Case of Priestly Intolerance at Roxton*. It appears that this refusal came about because the clergy had been told the child wasn't baptised – a fact that was then checked with her parents. The sexton who had tolled the bell to announce the death then admitted he would not have done so had he known! Deputations went to Gt. Barford to speak with the clergymen, who said they 'dare not bury her', but would have done so had they not been made aware of the facts. Despite waiting an hour beside the open grave, when no-one came to officiate the parents themselves buried the child in silence. 'The bell (comments the newspaper) was *not* tolled.' We are, like the writer of the published letter, left wondering why Rev. Rolls, Congregational Pastor, who resided in the village, did not step in to perform the burial rites? Perhaps there were boundaries that were not to be crossed in those days. [4]

A Plea for Help

There are few surviving records relating to the final quarter of the nineteenth century. We learn from H.G.Tibbutt that during the 1860's and 70's the Roxton Church was a member both of the Bedfordshire and the Huntingdonshire Unions of Christians.[5] That it was struggling to survive we can deduce from something that came to earth in the church papers. In February 1873 this leaflet asking for help was printed for general circulation to Independent worshippers in the locality. We have no record of whether it met with a successful response.

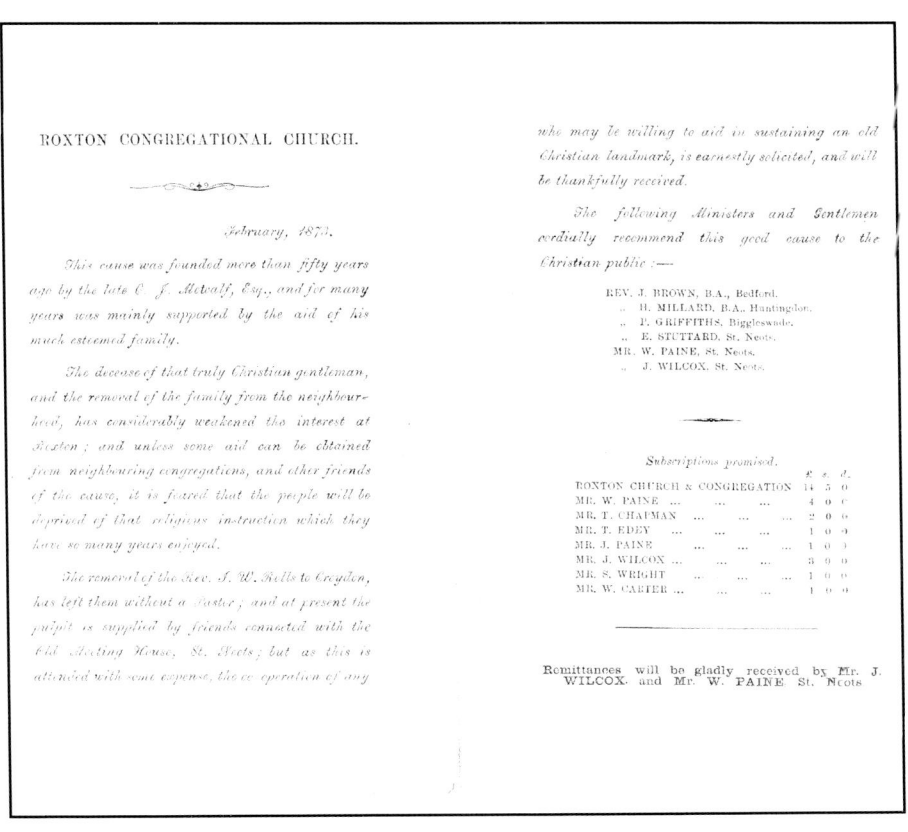

A Pamphlet dated February 1873, seeking support for Roxton Congregational Church.
Roxton Chapel

It reads:

> 'This cause was founded more than fifty years ago by the late C.J.Metcalf, Esq., and for many years was mainly supported by the aid of his much esteemed family. The decease of that truly Christian gentleman, and the removal of his family from the neighbourhood, has considerably weakened the interest at Roxton: and unless some aid can be obtained from the neighbouring congregations, and other friends of the cause, it is feared that the people will be deprived of that religious instruction which they have so many years enjoyed.
>
> The removal of the Rev. J.W.Rolls to Croydon, has left them without a Pastor; and at present the pulpit is supplied by friends connected with the Old Meeting House, St. Neots; but as this is attended at some expense, the co-operation of any who may be willing to aid in sustaining an old Christian landmark, is earnestly solicited, and will be thankfully received.'
>
> This proposal was endorsed by among others, Rev. J. Brown, B.A. Bedford and Messrs. W.Paine and J. Wilcox of St.Neots, who would 'gladly' receive remittances.

These were difficult times for the Church Meeting at Roxton. Rev. Rolls departed in 1872 after a period of twelve years, and a note in the church book states that for many years lay preachers came from the St. Neots Congregational Church. It was probably at this time that some families began to subsidise the church by paying rents for their pews. Not all could afford to, but those who were able to would pay an annual sum that guaranteed a basic income to the church. Consequently certain pews became identified with specific families; even now the pew on the left at the rear of the church is known as the King pew, and the raised pew, originally the Metcalfe pew was the Day pew and then became the Bath pew one hundred years ago when that family came to Roxton park. Pew rent continued to be paid by some families up to the 1940's.

Rev. James Gunn, previously minister at St. Neots, "watched over" Roxton until his departure for London in 1877. In 1886 the Bedford Union appointed Mr. Thomas Chapman, (a merchant and deacon from the St. Neots church) to Roxton, where he had formerly attended as a lay preacher.

*Thomas Chapman, pastor from 1886-1908, was formerly a merchant from St. Neots
Gibbs Collection*

It should be noted that in 1861 a Union of Christians was formed in Huntingdonshire, and for two decades the Roxton church was affiliated to both that and the Bedford Union.

Twelve years on, all seemed to be going well under his leadership; several joined the membership in 1888. In 1898, a report to the Bedford Union compiled under their Visitation Scheme referred to, 'surprisingly large congregations each evening, the chapel being nearly full, (with) a large attendance of young people'. A Mission Station had been opened at Chawston and services there were appreciated. The Roxton Sunday School 'was never better'. [5]

In the nineteen fifties, Thomas Chapman was recalled by older members and spoken of with the utmost respect and affection by members who knew him. Recounting their youthful experiences at Chapel they told of the happy times, when a huge number of young people gathered there. It was these people that were to become strong leaders of the Church as Society moved into the difficult days of the early 20th century.

A Late 19th Century Picture of the Chapel with very Overgrown Garden.
B. Hooker collection

A Congregational Church Tea c. 1895 Roxton W.I. Scrapbook; B.L.A.R.S. Ref. P28/28/1.

The St. Neots advertiser reported on the 12th July 1885:

> *Roxton Chapel Sunday School Anniversary 12-07-1885, Preacher John Brown*
>
> *The Sunday School Anniversary held this this week ...was altogether the most successful ...that has taken place for a long time. On Sunday, sermons were preached in the afternoon and evening by the well known Rev. John Brown of Bedford; the congregation on the latter occasion being altogether too large for the chapel which was filled to overflowing.......*
>
> *On Tuesday a Treat was given to the children in a field admirably adapted for the purpose loaned by Mr. Browning. In the evening (everyone) ...games were entered into with zest. The prizes, given by the Hunts. Association, were also distributed.*
>
> *The Sunday School has for the second year gained the prize of £3 awarded Roxton Congregational Church as to the school that passes the most scholars proportionately to the number on the role.'*

Thomas Chapman was to play a part in Christian fellowship at Roxton over many years, staying until the church celebrated its Centenary, however it is our loss that no records survive for the period of his ministry. Possibly few were ever kept and if he left this task to the Church deacons then sadly for us they failed in their duty. We learn from a later note in the Church register that James Bond was dismissed from membership in 1904 for having 'brought grave scandal upon the name of the Church (for which he) showed no penitence'. It is not for us to speculate on this judgement, but to note that at the same time he was admonished for failing in the upkeep of the registers 'in recent years'. It was 1904 when this oversight was discovered which rather indicates that all the deacons had neglected to check the records for some considerable time! It would seem that the records may not have been lost but simply neglected.

Changing Times

John Brown noting changes that took place towards the end of the nineteenth Century wrote 'we have to carry out our work under very different conditions from those under which our fathers carried on theirs....... First the social and economic changes in village life and the condition of agriculture have seriously affected the relations both of the Established Church and of the Free Churches to the people of the rural districts.

The fall in agricultural values affecting incomes.......and the reduction of the yeoman farmer class, once the strength of non-conformity and ....the steady decline of population in the villages.'[6] By the early 1870's farm labourers were forming themselves into unions, to better argue their cause. there is no evidence of a branch being formed at Roxton, but four hundred met to hear speeches at St.Neots in 1873 and a further four hundred met on the Vicarage lawn at Cople the following year where sixty labourers were said to be out of work. By contrast a letter received at Cardington from one of their people who had emigrated to New Zealand spoke of them doing quite well saying, 'we eat half a sheep a week' and told of much help from their new employer. The letter that went on to describe his new life must have seemed like an idyll to those who heard it.[7]

By 1901 the population of Roxton had dropped to nearly half its 1851 level, to stand at 349.

The Chapel at the turn of the 20^b century:　　　　　　　　　　　　*Gibbs collection*

Notes

1. Nigel E. Agar, *The Bedfordshire Farm Worker in the Nineteenth Century*, Bedfordshire Historical Record Society, vol.60, 1981, pp. 162-163

2. R. Steen, Nineteenth Century Voluntary Education Exemplified by Roxton National School, Bedfordshire. B.L.A.R.S.

3. H.G.Tibbutt, *The Dissenting Academies of Bedfordshire*, 111, Cotton End, Bedfordshire Magazine Autumn 1957, Vol. 6, No. 42, p.85

4. Roxton and District Local History Group graveyard plan 2002, row 21, grave D

5. H.G.Tibbutt, ibid, p.12

6. J. Brown B.A., D.D., *The History of the Bedfordshire Union* of Christians, London Independent Press Ltd.,1946, p81

7. Nigel Agar, *The Bedfordshire Farm Worker in the Nineteenth Century*, Bedfordshire Historical Record Society, Vol. 60, pp179, 190, 198

The Interior showing lighting by oil lamps- notice the front three sided pew.
B. Hooker collection

The Metcalfe Family- a Postscript

Following the sale of his estates in 1851/2, the house that was his home and sadly, even his chapel, Charles James Metcalfe lived out his final years at Roxton.[1] The village that he had called home for almost fifty years was where he wished to quietly spend his days, with Elizabeth and his two unmarried daughters at his side. The new owner, Robert Delap, who lived in Ireland had no need of the house and may have sympathised with Charles, allowing him to rent the property or even waiving rent altogether. The family in modern terms was destitute.

Countywide and beyond people would be talking about the serious financial position Charles Metcalfe was in. Gentlemen of the County with whom Charles Metcalfe had been on equal standing, rallied with support for their old friend. A deed dated 5th June 1854 shows that William Whitbread, Blyth Foster, Thomas Turnley and Henry Sewell raised £867.19s by subscription, which was invested for their friend and his immediate family in £3 percent consolidated annuities. This generosity afforded Charles and Elizabeth the means of a livelihood.

Charles Metcalfe Esq. died at his home and was buried in the family tomb in the graveyard at St. Mary Magdalene, Roxton on February 20th 1855. He was sixty nine years of age. He would have been remembered with respect and affection, not least among his many Christian friends in the Bedfordshire Union. John Brown writing later in 1896 claims 'Among other generous friends of the Union were all the members of the family of C.J.Metcalfe, Esq. of Roxton House who were true and steadfast through many years.' [2]

Also commemorated on the obelisk that marks his grave are his infant daughter, Katherine Affleck who died 16th March 1826; Frances, his second daughter who died 1st June 1840 and John May, his second son, who died February 25th 1841, aged 25 years, along with other family members.

The widowed Elizabeth then left the village. Her daughters went to the Continent to finish their education. The financial difficulties they now faced would have dramatically reduced Frances (Fanny) and Anna Sophia's prospects of marriage, and they realised that it was necessary for them to find a way of earning a living to enable them to support their mother. Much later in their lives they had occasion to tell their story: 'On our Father's death ...we had to face the world and we decided we would take up Education. ......We went abroad for seven years (there is a discrepancy here since they opened their school in 1858, just three years after the death of their father), and studied in Berlin and Paris'.

Charles Metcalfe and his family returned from Guernsey after a stay of only three years or so, but it seems that they did not return to this locality. He was in Guernsey in 1855, and Census records for 1861, when the family are back in England indicate that three of his sons were born in Guernsey. George Oswold, the youngest of these was born the year his Grandfather died. I have already suggested that Charles Jnr. came home for his father's funeral. We are left wondering whether the loss Charles James had suffered caused a tremendous strain in the relationship between father and son in those final years. In the 1861 Census returns Charles Metcalfe Jnr. gave his *means* (way of earning his living) as *Fundholder*.

Shortly after this he must have decided yet again, that having nothing to lose, he would take his family further afield to *pastures new*. New Zealand had only been settled by Europeans in the 1820's and had never been a penal colony. Immigration schemes had begun in the 1840's, but settlers were expected to purchase land on arrival, (unlike in Australia where land had been given to the settlers). Numbers arriving in New Zealand escalated dramatically in the 1860's after the discovery of gold in 1861. Charles and his family left from Gravesend on the *S.S.Tyburnia* on October 3rd. 1863. Since they are the first named on the passenger list we speculate that they travelled more comfortably than others; a considerable advantage since the voyage, which took them first to Tasmania, lasted for four months. The family arrived at Claremont Point on the Western coast early in 1864 where they settled at first, but by 1885 they had established their family at a newly built house at Matekohe where subsequent generations have farmed to the present day. It was at Matakohe that Charles Metcalfe Jn. and Alder Fisher went on to build a church. No doubt wishing to retain some link to their old home in England they named their new home and farm *Roxton*. Direct ancestors of the Metcalfe's of Roxton, England still farm there at the present time: they are decended from Charles and Louisa's son Morell, who was born in Guernsey in 1841. William Herbert, Charles' son, was to marry Elizabeth, the daughter of Alder Fisher at Matakohe.

A School for Gentlewomen

Fanny and Anna Sophia went on to establish a school for girls at Highfield, in Hendon, North London. The Metcalfe girls were successful in this venture - it is claimed to have been one of the largest schools of its kind in England. In 1869 Fanny became a member of the executive committee of Girton College, Cambridge and also a member of the Council of Westfield College, a position she held until her death. [3] She is interred at Hampstead, N. London.

Charles and Louisa returned to England later in their lives having left their young family to carry on farming in New Zealand. They are buried at Leamington.

Charles James' widow, Elizabeth, lived with her daughters in Hendon until her death in 1885 at the age of ninety-four. She was laid to rest with her husband in the family vault in the graveyard of Roxton Church. Her wish no doubt was, that she return to the village where she had spent her happiest years, and her body was brought by train from London to Tempsford station while a party of family mourners followed on the express train. That 'The old retainers of the Metcalfe family at Roxton met the *cortege* at Tempsford Station and acted as pallbearers' is indicative of the great affection in which she was held by those who knew her at Roxton. Five carriages brought local families, and an open car drove from London. 'Mr. Foster of Sandy Place.... although over 85, ... was taken in a bath chair to Sandy Station to see the coffin'.

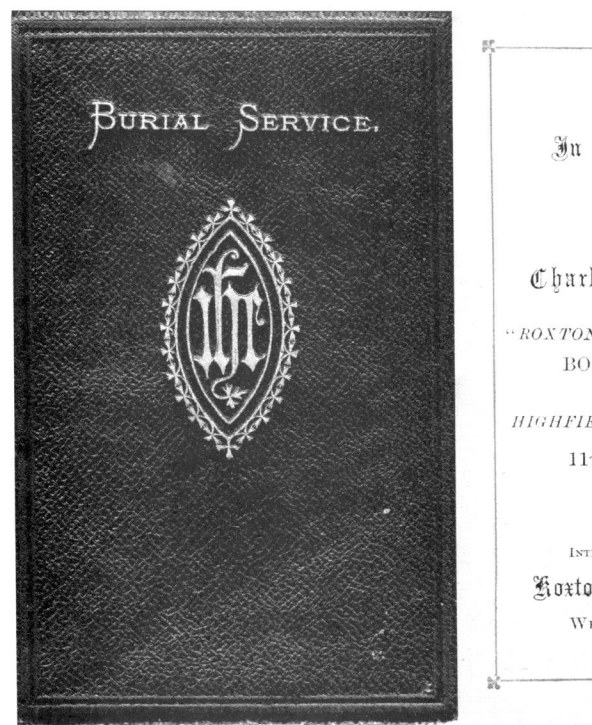
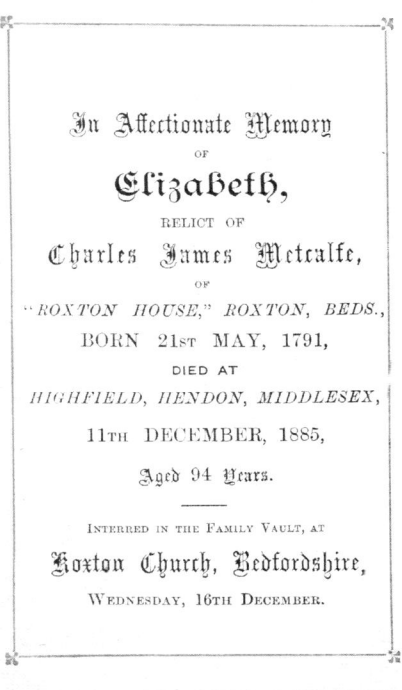

Funeral Service booklet for Mrs Elizabeth May Metcalfe. Published by Marshall and Snellgrove; Gibbs collection

We read, ' Awaiting at the (Parish) Church were between 200 and 300 persons' representing many local families - the wealthy seated beside the labouring classes who had all known and respected her. Mr. Edgar Winzar, most probably the son of their former pastor attended, as did so many others who had been close to the family forty or so years before. The Misses Metcalfe were 'embraced most warmly' by Mrs Bond Sen. who had formerly been their nurse. 'By the death of this venerable lady .... the greatest link which bound the Metcalfe family to the hearts of the people of Roxton had been severed.' [4]

In August 2007 Mr. Rodney Metcalfe a direct descendant of Charles James Metcalfe visited Roxton from New Zealand. He is pictured on the front cover. Other family members from Australia and England have visited the Chapel in recent years.

Notes.

1. Roxton Estate Sale Papers, B.L.A.R.S ref. X478/18-X478/61, Plan of Roxton Estate, ref. X468/20.

2. J. Brown B.A., D.D., The History of the Bedfordshire Union of Christians, London Independent Press   Ltd., p.80

3. G. Metcalfe member no Hatch 3, www.metclafe family society, cites Educational Review, July & Aug
1890 pp.117-118; London Times 11th July 1897 p.6.

4. The Bedfordshire Mercury December 1885.

The Gilbert family were a Chapel family with six recorded members C1900: Fred (back right)Deacon and Gardener; Thomas (we believe back left) Deacon, S.S teacher and Treasurer. Mrs John Gilbert is shown with her five sons and three daughters

*The Livett family worshipped at Chapel ; Sam Livett, is back row, second from left.
Roxton W.I. Scrapbook; B.L.A.R.S. Ref P28/28/1.*

The Early 20th Century

The Chapel as the Centre of Many Lives

H.G.Tibbutt writing in 1958 stated that the Church Book for the years 1873-1901 had been missing for almost half a century and consequently little was known of events at Roxton between those years. However it would seem that in the 1950's no-one could remember seeing the book and I have suggested that records were not kept efficiently. Reports to the Bedfordshire Union in 1901 noted that 'seven of the Sunday School scholars had certificates awarded for Biblical Knowledge and one gained first prize.' [1]

The Chapel in the early years of the 20th Century   *Gibbs collection*

In 1904, after a lapse of thirty years, records began again in a new Church Book. Its gold - printed title:-

Records of the Congregational Church Assembling at Roxton.

The membership which had suffered a serious decline through death and no doubt many lapses in attendance now stood at twenty three. From 1886 Thomas Chapman had been leading the church and although he came from St. Neots it seems that he resided in Roxton, at least in the later years of his ministry. At the time of the 1901 Census, then aged 74, he is lodging with Rebecca Barcock, a widow, and her daughter, Maud in New Row. Although his health was declining Mr. T. Chapman was still ministering to the church and was respected by everyone. Times had changed and joyful participation in worship and the affairs of the church had replaced the more earnest devotions of former decades. Congregations grew and the church community became central to the lives of many of the people of the village. Their social life as well as their Christian life revolved around their Chapel; that was the name by which they knew the Congregational Church.

The children who had enrolled in Mr. Chapman's popular Sunday School were to become the young people who flocked to the services and became an important part of the church community, many taking up membership.

The Chapel Ladies Serve Tea.

Teas began to be quite an event in the church calendar and a set of bone china engraved with a line drawing of the Chapel was bought during Mr. Chapman's ministry. Members were able to order some pieces privately and some local families still own pieces. Some pieces of the china are still held by the Church but are far too fragile to use. Records show that in 1906, 'it was resolved to resume the annual New Year Tea'. The late George A. Bambridge recalled New Year teas from his childhood in the early 20th century, when a Christmas Tree decorated the schoolroom and Freddie Bath, disguised as Father Christmas, arrived through the South porch, to everyone's delight! Gifts from under the tree were distributed to the excited children, before games and singing were organised in the vestry. A copper boiler dates from this period—it must have given good service helping to quench many thirsts after robust hymn singing! There was an annual Choir tea, a New Year tea that coincided with the annual Member's Meeting.

A Sunday School Anniversary tea, called a Treat, was held on Tuesday following the anniversary. Members have recalled these Summer picnic teas when everyone sat on matting on the grass near the pond, and willow laundry baskets full of sandwiches and cake were carried round to everyone. Mrs. T. Bambridge told of what a treat this was, since as children of labourers they were only allowed to have either jam or butter on their bread at teatime, never both!

The Early 19th Century banners that were awarded for Chapels with the best choir were presented to the Chapel and have been held since that time. They hang in the Schoolroom today.

S. Eldridge

Bone China, Transfer Printed, Chapel Tea Service dated approx.1900
S. Eldridge

The Bedfordshire Times reported on September 6th 1901 that over one hundred sat down to an afternoon tea, probably held outside, which was free to everyone over sixty. The company often spilled over into Chapel Close, the meadow adjacent to the Chapel. It is worth noting that water would previously have been fetched from the village pump that was supplied by a natural underground source. The old village pump could still be seen on the verge opposite the chapel into the mid-twentieth century; by this time however clean water was piped throughout the village and a standpipe was positioned on the green opposite the adjacent cottages.

Centenary—a Time for Celebration

In 1908 the Centenary was celebrated. For the occasion the building had been thoroughly renovated by skilled local craftsmen and members. The receipt from J. Brimley is for £29.7.0.

> £29 = 7 = 0   5th May 1908
>
> I hereby agree for the sum of Twenty nine pounds seven shillings - to carry out the renovation of Roxton Chapel according to the specifications and to the satisfaction of Mr J. Brimley Roxton by the   day of May 1908: one pound per day to be allowed off for every day taken over that time

A receipt for work carried out prior to the Centenary Celebration
Chapel collection

On Whit Sunday crowded congregations heard Rev. Dr. Garvie, principal of New College, London preach. Following an afternoon service at which Rev. C. Piggott of Bunyan Meeting preached, three hundred sat down to a celebration Public Tea in James Day's Tithe Barn. That evening a Christian public meeting was held with local ministers from St. Neots, Eynesbury and the chairman of the Beds. Union of Christians taking part.

The following Sunday after serving the church for twenty-two years, the aged Thomas Chapman resigned his duties. James Day also resigned as deacon – he expected to leave the village by September of 1908. Loyal members, Caleb Covington, John Gilbert and John King assumed the role of Church Committee. The Beds Union were once again there to give advice, and upon their recommendation Rev. James Hammil of Kettering was invited to the Pastorate. Services and a tea were held to mark the start of his ministry in October 1909, an evening public meeting being presided over by E.T. Leeds Smith Esq. of Sandy. At the meeting, which commanded a large attendance, addresses were given by Christian gentlemen from Potton, Blunham and Roxton, included among them Wm. Browne of Sandy, who was a well known and popular evangelising speaker.

Worship and Christian Social Activity c1910

Classes were held for the Sunday School and for Mutual Improvement, (a youth group perhaps?) and there is the first mention of a Sunday School Anniversary to be held on July 10th when three services were held. A children's Treat followed on Tuesday when over two hundred adults and children sat down to tea. This was Summer time, so afterwards 'games and cricket were indulged in until late evening', no doubt in Mr. Brown's field which came to be known as Chapel Close.

Music had become a Chapel tradition by this time and a choir led by Mr. Wm. George Simcoe attracted the young and old, with the men singing bass or tenor parts. Miss E. Simcoe, daughter of the choir leader had a lovely soprano voice, and trained by her father she often took the soprano lead or solo part. Special Christian music was purchased for concerts and performances. The choir gave **Services of Song** both in the Chapel and at nearby village chapels too.

Miss E. Simcoe, (later Mrs. F. Gilbert), soloist and the front cover of a music book used for the Services of Song; Gibbs collection

A Sunday School Treat; probably in Chapel Close, the little meadow adjacent to the Chapel, c 1900 Roxton W.I.Scrapbook, held at B.L.A.R.S.

Mrs. Gilbert recounted how they had all enjoyed these occasions, when the whole choir walked to Gt. Barford, Tempsford, Blunham and Wyboston on Summer evenings. Anthems were prepared and sung at special services. Many cottages housed a harmonium and hymns were practised and sung at home by Christian families. Mrs. Clay the wife of the village baker who taught the village children to play the piano was one of the organists at this time, the others being Miss Kitty Ekins and Mrs. King. Ten years later Mrs. Sarah Jefferies and then Miss Gertrude Hull also helped with accompaniment, Mrs King having retired in 1917.

A local newspaper reported in 1914:

> *The Congregationalists of the village should be proud of their choir, who began the New Year by rendering a service of song entitled, "Won by a Song". The connective readings were given by the new pastor, the Rev. R. Harmstone, B.A. The solo "Oh Golden Day" was taken by Mrs. F. Gilbert. This effort was in aid of the annual choir tea, which took place on Monday evening.'*

Harvest decorations c1910. The balcony with highly decorated clock, festoons and oil lamps   Gibbs collection

Harvest Thanksgiving services were held later one hundred years ago. That year on October 9th and a sale of harvest produce had been established on the following Monday evening.

Band of Hope Meetings

The Band of Hope movement's aim was to strongly exhort the danger of drink. It preached that alcohol was the scourge of society and this message was spread through Christian meetings. Members were encouraged to abstain from drinking and were then asked to commit to a life of abstinence from alcohol by *Signing the Pledge*. In late life one member, known to the author, who had committed to this pledge in their youth, had kept that promise.

In December that year, condolences were sent to Wm. Addington, Church Warden of St. Mary Magdalene, on the death of Rev.Wm. Brown. His response included the hope that, 'kindly feelings between the two churches may always exist.'

Much fuller minutes provide us with a detailed picture of Church life early in the 20th century. We learn that it was customary to hold an annual Service of Celebration of the Ejected Ministers of 1662; that subscriptions were paid to a central Congregational Fund; money was raised for the London Missionary Society through a tea and entertainment held on Easter Monday in 1912 and a series of Mission Services were held on consecutive evenings that Spring. A Bath Chair was purchased from funds for the use of the aged Rev. Hamill and other infirm villagers. His death is recorded in July 1913. Thereafter local preachers supplied the pulpit, but an understandable request was made to The Union, that '*a young man*' be sought for the pastorate. Having lost two elderly pastors in quick succession the members were keen to avoid a further similar occurrence.

Mr. and Mrs. F. Bath, new tenant farmers at the Roxton Estate came to the village in 1908 and joined the fellowship in 1913 and actively supported the church and its community, Mrs Bath giving a set of cups and tray for use in the Communion of the Lord's Supper. New lights provided better light, especially over the pulpit, which was still at the rear of the church. (See picture on next page)

Rev. Harmstone begins his Pastoral Duties

In February 1914 Rev. R. Harmstone, a former student from Cheshunt College, left his church at Spalding to begin his ministry at Roxton. That year concerns were raised about the state of the building - the thatch needed attention and the west end was showing signs of settlement – and also whether there was adequate fire insurance cover.

*The Chapel Interior showing the new lights and new stove installed in 1914.
B. Hooker collection*

The building, still owned by Mr. Delap as part of the Roxton Estate was hired to the membership at a *peppercorn rent* of one shilling a year, but members were concerned about the future security of their place of worship should ownership of the estate change. Written assurances were obtained that the chapel would be rebuilt if it suffered a fire and deacons took out insurance against damage to the interior furniture and fittings.

The Darkest of Times, – WW1

Following the Union Spring Meeting of 1914, Rev. Hiley spoke of a note of despair in the newspapers. That was two months before hostilities began. The Great War was seen as a righteous war and from Congregational pulpits tribute was paid to the thousands of young men who were at the Front. [2] This included the many young men from Roxton and the Chapel.

Food restrictions affected the population although less severely in the countryside, and the cost of living increased.

Rev. Harmstone and Mrs. Bath assembled goods that were packed and sent to the men fighting in France; Chapel ladies were busily knitting balaclava helmets, socks and gloves and these were parcelled up with the food and tobacco.

In 1915 Rev. T. Chapman was laid to rest in the Churchyard at Roxton as Rev. Hamill had been two years previously [3]

Two of the Chapel Young Men who paid the Ultimate Price.

No mention is made of the war at the annual meeting in January 1915, but several present would have been quietly concerned, knowing that their sons were at the front. Late in the war Joseph Simcoe had gone to the Front. He and his wife Edith had become members only in 1916. His father sent postcards of the chapel to his son and to Alfred Covington at the Front.

The understated message reveals his deep love for his son through the mutual affection in which both hold the Chapel, which he calls 'the ole place'. The message however assumes a far greater poignancy as we learn that it was returned to the father after his son was killed, possibly having never even been received. Private Covington also sent a similar postcard back to his Mother before his death. His father G. Caleb Covington, long time deacon and Sunday School Teacher, died in December 1915 and thus was spared the knowledge that two of his three sons would die in France the following year. (*www. Beds Archives ref. Z291/656/32*) Sadly, his daughter Edith Rosina who was married to Joseph Simcoe would soon learn that she too was widowed.

William George Simcoe's words to his son Joseph:

> 'Dear Friend, I have sent you this card to remind you of the ole place where I know you would love to be and I trust you will soon be again. I thought you would like to show some of your friends the old place, so I have sent you the outside and the inside. Show your mates where your seat is......I am looking for the time to come when we shall have you home again... with very best love from your ole friend, Geo Simcoe.'

It is doubtful that they were ever read.

Corporal Joseph Simcoe, and the postcard sent to him at the front by his father W. G. Simcoe

The following letter, sent to Edith Rosina, Joseph Simcoe's wife, was published in the St. Neots Advertiser.

> *Dear Madam,*
>
> *I regret to inform you of the death of your husband, Lce.Corpl.J.Simcoe (Bedfords) who was killed April 17th by a German sniper. ......I was sorely grieved when I was told about it. Some time ago we had given each other our addresses, so as to let those at home know if anything did happen. I found him a good and true Christian, many times he had told me of the good times he had spent at his Chapel and we often passed an hour reading a portion of Scripture or singing hymns.*
>
> *He ends with a Christian message and his signature Lance.Corpl. B.T.Barrett (Bedfords).*

Many of these sons of Roxton were laid in unmarked graves on a *Foreign Field* – and families at home quietly mourned their loss.

Some village men who had answered the call to fight with courage and conviction, returned gassed, wounded and emotionally scarred but speaking little of the horror of they had witnessed or the friends that were left in France; among them W.T.Bambridge, F. Gadsden, J.W. Gilbert, F. Brace, Herbert Covington, G. Darrington, J. Ekins, J. Jefferies and W. King. These listed here are just those known to have been associated with the Chapel. One Roxton man interviewed in the 1980's spoke sadly of when he returned from France all those years ago saying that all his mates were left behind, and the village was never the same again.

Church Life apparently carried on; Rev Harmstone took over as Pastor in 1914; delegates were sent to the annual meeting of the Bedfordshire Union of Christians and the Church participated in the local exchange of ministers annually in June. In 1916 some long serving officers had relinquished their tasks; organist Mrs. King retired due to failing eyesight and Kitty Ekins took over; Thomas Gilbert assumed the Treasurer's role from John King; T. Jefferies became Church Secretary.

William George Simcoe, choirmaster 1907-1917 resigned his membership in 1917. Although this was one month before the recorded date of the death of his son in France, like many ordinary people he was probably deeply shocked by the news from France; already three young men from the chapel whom he

Roxton Chapel Roll of Honour

S. Eldridge

Men commemorated on the Congregational Church Roll of Honour

The Church Rook records this dedication,

'The following young men connected with this Church laid down their lives in the Great War.'

Darrington. Peter   1st July 1916
Private, 7th Bedfordshire Regt.
Battle of the Somme

Covington. Alfred John   30th July 1916
Lance Corporal, 7th Bedfordshire Regt.

Covington. Wilfred   12th Oct. 1916
Private, 7th Bedfordshire Regt.

Simcoe. Joseph.   18th April 1917
Lance Corporal, 8th Bedfordshire Regt.

Gilbert. John William   9th May 1917
Private, 1st. East Surrey Regt.

Ekins. Albert Walter   6th May 1917
Observer Royal Flying Corps. Germany

Darrington. Alfred   21st Nov. 1917
Lance Corporal, Gloucestershire Regt.

had known so well had been killed, and he probably anticipated the same fate might befall his son. Already widowed he must have become very depressed and suffered a crisis in his Faith. The records state 'Ceased attending Chapel' against his name. He was ill for almost two years before his death in 1919, which is not recorded in the register.

Albert Ekins, who took over as choir master, asked if the minister could attend the weekly practice 'so that *harmony* might prevail.'! Not vocal harmony we suspect but possibly he envisaged problems at the sudden loss of the choristers' former choirmaster, or perhaps because the membership had voted to adopt The Congregational Praise as the new hymn book.

William George Simcoe, gardener and Choirmaster
Gibbs collection

Welcome Home and a 'Stiff Upper Lip'.

The St. Neots' Advertiser reported on a **Soldiers' Welcome Home Tea:-**

> 'A Soldiers "Welcome Home" was held in the schoolroom on Saturday last. The arrangements were made by the Parish Council working through a committee which represented the whole village. Each ex-serviceman was asked to bring one friend to a high tea. The guests were welcomed by the Clerk and at the close of the meal kind reference to the memory of the fallen was made by the Vicar. Those taking part in the concert were the Misses Wilkerson and friends, Mrs. Bath, Miss Dennison, Messrs. Hayman, Jones, Papworth, Thorn and Dalton .... The accompanists were Mrs. Brown, Mrs. Clay and Miss Whitchurch. After a few well-chosen words by the Chairman and Mr. Whitchurch the company dispersed.'

At this time the Chapel Anniversary was always celebrated during January with a special service and a tea. One week night following, an entertainment was arranged; Mr. Poynter's Lantern-Slide Lectures on a Christian theme were always popular. We must remember that these were the days before television and it was a good opportunity for a social evening out! George A. Bambridge recalled that Mr. Poynter went to all the chapels and talked on Temperance. His signature tune went as follows;

> 'Dare to be a Daniel, Dare to Stand Alone, Dare to pass a Public House and Take your Money Home!'

Local Evangelists brought their caravan mission to Chapel Close every year; they also preached temperance; *Gibbs collection*

Making Ends Meet in the Early 20th Century.

Church Rules were revisited in 1919 and since most new members had no knowledge of the rules drawn up in 1842 the Minister was asked to draw up a new list. Whether he did we do not know- no list is placed on record! His stipend which was set at £120 per annum was proving difficult to raise, and had to be supplemented by addition of the Harvest offering. Roof repairs costing £13.12.00 were necessary in 1920 and Mr. Lewin of Tempsford undertook the work. A Jumble Sale was planned to offset some of this expense. In 1924 new lamps were bought to be paid for by a Sale of Work organised by the ladies under leadership of Mrs. Bath. Mrs Brace, caretaker for twenty years died in 1921 and Lydia Livett, took over for the coming years; her salary was £4 per annum. The roof had been repaired late in 1920/1921 by Mr. Lewin of Tempsford. At the annual Church meeting 'It was resolved that the cost of same, £13.12.00, be met by a Jumble Sale to be held on the last Saturday in February'.

Mr Fred Bath

How splendid the newly thatched Chapel looked c. 1927   *Gibbs collection*

No major work had been carried out on the building for many years and the thatch was in a sorry state when in 1927 Mr. F. Bath had reed brought from Norfolk and paid for the complete re-thatching.

Sunday School Treats

Chapel life was an integral part of the social life of the village and in the summer of 1923 many would have turned out for the joint Church and Chapel Treat. Villagers would have crowded to see the procession of floral-decorated cycles and perambulators and hoops that progressed from the Chapel School via the main street, to the Park where everyone was welcomed by Mrs. Bath. The tea was held on the chapel lawns and followed by races and games in the adjacent park. Fun was had at Mr. Wilson's coconut shy, set up for the day, and the Salvation Army band enlivened the atmosphere. The finale was always a scramble for sweets scattered all around on the grass by long serving Sunday School teachers, John King and Thomas Gilbert. The fun of these simple celebrations is still remembered!

Sunday School at this time was held in the morning at the same time as the morning service. Adults attended morning worship returning home for their Sunday lunches. Not every cottage had an oven and for a couple of pence Mr. Clay, the village baker would cook the joint in his huge bread oven. We might wonder how he determined which joint belonged to a particular customer however people were glad of this service, and this practice continued well into the 20th century. His bakery was situated on the little green at the south of the main street.

Rev. Harmstone ended his ten year ministry at Roxton in July 1924, to take up ministry in St. Ives, Cornwall at the Countess of Huntingdon's Zion Church. It was the end of an era and little wonder that resignations of deacons ensued. Despite petitions that such resignations were 'inappropriate and inadvisable' the former officers did not desist and Mr. F. Bath and Miss E. Ekins took over as Treasurer and Secretary respectively.

Notes

1. H.G.Tibbutt, Roxton Congregational Church 1808-1958, p. 14.

2. D. Prothero, B.A., B.Sc., B.D. The History of the Bedfordshire Union of Christians Part 11, The Story Continued, p.117

3. Roxton and District Local History Group, Graveyard Survey, 2002 p. 15 respectively graves 16A and 16B.

Twenty Years with Faithful Leadership, 1925- 1945

The proposal put by the Moderator of the Beds Union, at a Special Meeting, that Roxton members consider a union between their church and Blunham Baptist Church under one Minister, must have met with strong resistance. After discussion a vote against was recorded and plans to continue independently were forged. It was resolved to hire 'The Bungalow' (the present day Hope Cottage) as a better minister's residence and the following year Rev. Slater of Irchester agreed to take over pastoral duties for one year and live part-time there. He was to lead the Roxton Fellowship for eight years, retiring in 1933.

When the Roxton Estate was put on the market by Major Delap around 1925 the Bath family were able to purchase the farm that they had hitherto rented. They then assumed ownership of the Chapel, which in 1925 they generously gifted to the Congregational Union of England and Wales. That same year the exterior of the building was badly in need of decoration and Mr. Bath generously settled the bill for this work, then in 1928 we read 'it had been necessary to re-roof the building' and a deficit was carried over on the balance sheet. A new method of fund raising was needed and members and friends were asked to hold a fund-raising box at home which could encourage contributions. The boxes scheme was very successful and continued for a number of years.

A full report of the Harvest Festival is a rare thing in the Church records but fortunately in 1929 we read, 'this year was memorable in many ways. In spite of the long drought during which vegetation was scorched and withered and produce from the garden and field alike, very scarce, we had a magnificent collection of flowers, fruit, vegetables and other good things brought together by our people' and during the afternoon, 'thanksgiving boxes' for the church funds were collected. A total of £26.00 was realised when the income from the Harvest sale was added.

Christian Social Meetings

That autumn, **Pleasant Friday Evening** meetings were started at which Christian entertainment; choral renditions, solos, recitations, recitals and the occasional lantern - slide show took place, always accompanied by an address. Anyone over fifteen could attend and the meetings proved to be popular and profitable. Mr. F. Darrington was the mainstay of the meetings, which continued for many years. He acted as treasurer while Mrs. Ethel Holden was secretary. One meeting in the 1930's was specifically remembered; Miss Nancy Holden had sung a solo which was illustrated dramatically by old Mrs. Hannah Matthews, then aged over 90, who sat beside the soloist quietly rocking in her chair. Mr Poynter also entertained with his religious magic lantern slides. 'Tommy' Jefferies and 'Frank' Darrington are remembered for duets including *Simply Trusting Every Day* and *Jesus keep me near the Cross*. A charge of one penny a week was made to attend, and then at the end of the winter season each young person was given a book.

Marjorie King began service as an Organist, Christian commitment that was to span the years 1926-1990, albeit with breaks when her family was growing up; Gosling family collection

An Annual Meeting which continued for fifty or so years was held in support of the London Missionary Society, and missionaries who were retired or home on leave came to preach and tell of their experiences. In 1925 'a memorable meeting' was addressed by a former missionary to Madagascar and on another occasion Annie Bone who had been a missionary to Algiers preached. Mrs Marjorie Gosling recounted her Mother's stories: she had attended a meeting at which a memorable address had been given by Marianne Farringdon, writer of the hymn, *'Just as I am Thine own to be'*. Village collections were taken for Mission work during the mid-nineteenth century and support is still given for mission work, through the Congregational Federation.

During Mr. Slater's ministry the first Chapel Outing was held to Wicksteed Park. Apparently on the way home a stop was made at the *Flower Pot P.H*. Bedford. Can we believe that note in the Church book I wonder?

Chapel members enjoy outings to Wicksteed Park and the seaside during the 1930's; Gibbs and Hooker collections

Sunday School Activities and Long Serving Teachers Honoured

From the Sunday School accounts which begin in 1921 we learn much of the activities organised for the children. Music sheets were purchased, prizes for the Children's tea on July 12th and other items.

December	*1920*	*Prize books*		*£1.18.16*
March	*1921*	*Mr. Clay (the village baker)*	*bread and cakes*	*£1.9.0*
March	*1921*	*C.E.Ekins*	*sugar and tea*	*£0.1.8*
March	*1921*	*Mrs A.E.King*	*butter*	*£0.7.0*
July	*1927*	*C.E.Ekins*	*cakes and biscuits*	*No price recorded*
April	*1927*	*Mrs. Livett*	*washing tablecloths*	*£0.2.0*
July	*1927*	*Mrs.Bath*	*prizes for racing*	*£0.1.0*

Books cost £1-6-6, and presents from under the Christmas Tree £1.5.0 in the same year.

The following year the meeting reported a 'revival of life and activity' within the church community. Miss E. King was Treasurer and she and Mr. Alfred King, Deacons. Mr. John King was Sunday school Superintendant (Sunday School was held in the morning at that time). Mrs F. Bath presided at a fortnightly Band of Hope meeting.

A Free Church Branch of The League of Nations was formed at the Church in 1927. Its aim was to support those who were fighting and through education to work towards the prevention of any future war. It seems to have been a lively, well supported group, with many of the Church members taking up membership. Miss Lawrence was secretary while Mrs Bath acted as treasurer and the chair was taken by Mr. John King. Meetings were held and special speakers engaged. An open air meeting was planned for the summer and singing practice held in preparation for this, but eventually an autumn meeting that replaced it attracted sixty people. Hymn sheets and 'bills', advertising the event were produced. In June 1928 Rev. D.S.Bonsall addressed an open air meeting on 'The Peace Ideal'. Other addresses were on similar themes; 'Blessed are the Peacemakers'; 'Put up thy Sword into thy Sheath'. The group eventually merged with another local branch and as history tells, the ideals espoused by the movement were ultimately to be of little consequence.

In 1930, learning that the lease of the bungalow where the minister resided was running out, members met and after serious debate, 'resolved to take steps towards building a manse.' These were ambitious plans but their hopes were soon dashed when the response to their request to the Union for a loan, elicited 'little encouragement!' Their problem was resolved by Mrs. Bath who offered to adapt rooms in Park Gate Cottage for the use of a Pastor.

The meeting also reported that the outstandingly long service of Sunday School Superintendent John King, (40 years) and Teacher Thomas Gilbert, (27 years), had been recognised by the Bedford District Sunday School Union. Each had been awarded certificates to mark their long service at a presentation ceremony in Bedford on April 24th 1929.

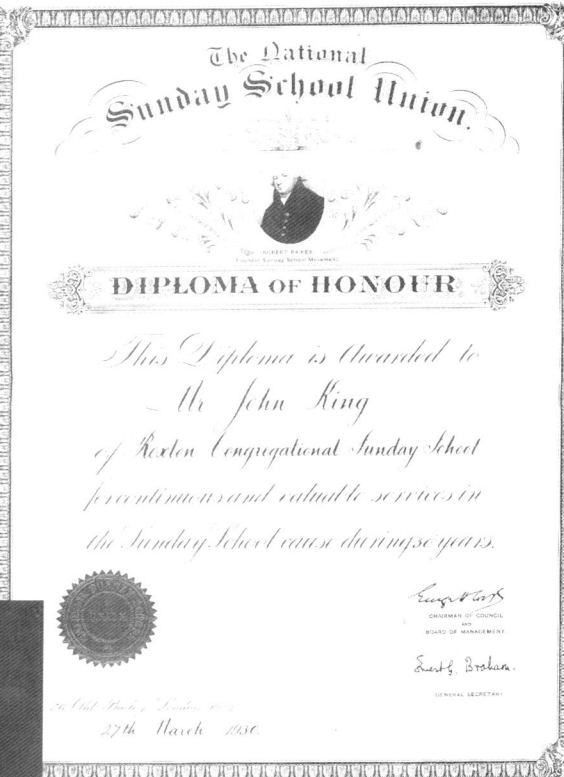

John King long serving Sunday school Superintendent and the Diploma of Honour awarded to him in recognition of forty years' service ; Gosling family collection.

At the annual Church meeting in 1931 the highest membership figure since 1861 was recorded. Six new members having joined the membership during the preceding year the total now stood at 49, and record congregations were also noted; an average of 40 attending Sunday mornings and 58 at the evening services.

Fire on a Pleasant Friday Evening

Alas, the new thatch was to suffer damage when during one of the Pleasant Friday Evening meetings on October 30th 1931, while Rev. Slater was giving an address, 'sparks were seen to fall from the above...(and) it was quickly realised that the roof was on fire!' The flue from the stove must have become very hot and ignited the thatch. The dramatic secretary's report continues that the building was evacuated, and 'the men present rushed for ladders and the women for pails of water'. In no time, 'men were on the roof dashing water on the flames'. Chemical extinguishers 'were rushed down from Roxton House and discharged on the (thatched) bell tower' and no doubt to great relief, 'the flames were subdued'. A postscript adds wryly, 'St. Neots Firemen arrived after the flames had been thoroughly quenched!' The insurers paid out £100 for redecoration which also facilitated the installation of electric lighting and heating.

Pleasant Friday Evening programme for the night of the fire
Gibbs collection

Yes! It's Starting Again!
ROXTON P.F.E.
opens a New Session

On FRIDAY, OCTOBER 9th, 1931.

Opening Address by Mrs. Filewood
(of Sandy)

Recitals by Rev. E. Slater.

Other Meetings:

Oct. 16th. J. A. WHITCHURCH, Esq., J.P.
    23rd. Rev. Dr. ASHTON (of China).
    30th. ~~SOCIAL EVENING~~. *Chapel caught fire*
Nov. 6th. Mrs. HAMMIL (of Sandy).
    13th. Lieut.-Col. HOGG (of Bedford).
           League of Nations Meeting.
    20th. Rev. W. RICHARDSON (Blunham)
    27th. ~~Rev. E. SLATER~~. *Social Evening — People from Bedford*

We are in for a good Session.
Come on Oct. 9th and join us.

Let those join up who never joined before,
And those who have joined, come and join once more.

Printed by J. F. Cook, Church, Rushden.

The Autumn meeting of the Bedfordshire Union 1932

In 1933 the Rev. Slater held the office of President of the Union and the Church at Roxton Church was honoured to host the Union Autumn Meeting. On September 14th delegates assembled from all over the county. It was, stated the record, 'a glorious day' continuing by noting the visitor's delight at seeing 'our unique sanctuary'. Luncheon and tea were served and speeches of thanks given, which were responded to by Mrs Bath, Miss King and Rev. Slater. It was a day recalled with joy and pride by the late Mrs. F. Gilbert. Naturally this was an occasion for the ladies of the church to wear their *Sunday Best* on a weekday, and all glowed with pride when visitors delighted to see the Roxton Church. 'Many expressions of delight on seeing our unique little sanctuary were heard on every hand', wrote Miss King, the secretary, and 'warm expressions of gratitude for hospitality were responded to by Mrs. Bath, Miss King and the Rev. Slater.'

The Christian World Visits Roxton

The Christian World newspaper reported on a visit to Roxton on May 31st 1934, when Rev. Rowland took over the pastorate:

> 'Roxton Church is one of the most remarkable and beautiful of countryside churches. In ground cut out of the park by the gift of the Metcalfe family 126 years ago and lovingly tended ever since, a barn was dedicated for Congregational worship and with great taste and skill transformed into a cruciform building whose transepts are small schoolrooms. Reed - thatch decends all round to wide eaves supported by rustic pillars, half-hidden by ivy or honey-suckle.'

'Tea was provided for a company that overflowed into the grounds' at a service to welcome the new minister, the Bedfordshire Times and Independent reported. The St. Neots Avertiser reported that Rev. Rowland's church at Shanghai sent a £2 donation to the Roxton Church. In his autobiography, Alfred Rowland D.D., LL.B., B.A. stated that he had retired many years earlier but speaks of the temporary pastorates that he undertook during the succeeding years. Amazingly it seems that he ministered to the church at Roxton throughout the ninety-fourth and ninety-fifth years of his life, until October 1935. His autobiography is signed, 'In remembrance of much kindness, the blazing summer of 1934. A.H.R.'.

*Rev. Alfred Norman
Rowland M.A.
1934-1935
Gibbs collection*

Close Links with Bunyan Meeting and Rev. Prothero's Ministry

A minute in the Church Book that we may all too easily identify with in modern times, states, 'Our expenses are more, we find the electric light and heaters very expensive!'

Mr. K.G. Jefferies was elected as a fourth deacon in 1935 to serve with Mrs Bath, Mr. J. King and Miss N. Holden. Close links were retained with Bunyan Meeting church and Rev. D. Prothero of Bedford preached at the Sunday School Anniversary on July 14th. (*The time of this anniversary on the second Sunday of July, is the same day as the traditional day of Roxton Feast – a village event that died out at the time of WW1.*) The Chapel celebrated its anniversary in April that year and a charabanc brought people from Bunyan Meeting to an afternoon service. After tea everyone enjoyed a choral religious musical performance by a Bedford choir.

That year £14.2s.2d the total proceeds of the Harvest collection and sale of produce, auctioned in the schoolroom 'on Monday by Mr. P. Bath', (was) sent to the Bedford County Hospital. Rev. Rev. D. Prothero B.A., B.D., B.Sc., who was a schoolmaster at Bedford Modern School and had also acted as assistant minister to the village churches of the Bedfordshire Union for the previous ten years, took up the ministry at Roxton in 1936. His appointment was heralded by reports in the Bedfordshire newspapers. It was marked by a special afternoon service of induction on Tuesday of Easter week 1937.

Rev. David Prothero B.A., B.D., B.SC. Minister at Roxton, 1936-1947.

This was followed by a 7pm meeting during which the Bedford Polychordia, accompanied by Mr. Colson, organist of St.Paul's, Bedford, gave a concert. The day was an occasion for celebration and another Public Tea was held - no doubt between the services. There were, the newspaper tells us, many visitors from Bedford and 150 sat down. Donations received for the tea were used to buy 'much needed new carpet for the platform and pulpit.' It is still giving good service today!

The Church Records remind us that the Coronation of King George 6th took place on May 12th that year. Mr. & Mrs Prothero, who continued to live at Bedford, came to join the village celebrations, which were held at the Park, where games were organised and afterwards, refreshments served in the big glasshouse.

During Rev. Prothero's ministry, close links were again fostered between Bunyan Meeting and Roxton churches; joint meetings were held at Roxton and the Bedford British Women's Group met here. Mrs. Prothero, who became busily involved with the Church, started the Women's Guild which seems to have been the first women's meeting to be held at the Church. In 1938 Bunyan members came to Roxton Church Anniversary in a charabanc. There was an afternoon service followed by tea, and a choral evening performance.

In the early months of Rev. Prothero's ministry there were several gifts to the church; the Lawrence family gave a brass lectern in memory of their parents; Miss E.E.King gave two Adam chairs in memory of her brother Alfred, and Mrs Prothero gave a brass flower vase.

Worth noting from the 1941 statement of accounts is that the minister's stipend (salary) was £85.0.0 with £10.7.0 added for travelling expense. Families were still paying rent for their pews to support the church. Total income for that year was £203.1.7. Electricity and insurance were the next greatest expense at around £17.0.0 each. Balancing the financial books was a continual problem, in the mid-1930's grants received from the Congregational Union reduced by more than half to £20.00, and that received from the Bedford Union by one third to £10.00. The demand on church finances seemed greater than the income and Rev. Prothero agreed to take less stipend, saying he 'could not have good work hindered by money worries'.

A Second Threat of Fire

On the evening of Tuesday May 18th, 'a terrific thunderstorm passed over Roxton and Mr. W. Jefferies saw 'a flash of lightning strike the (thatched) belfry tower'. As flames leapt from the thatch he ran to the street and shouted to raise the alarm. His cries of 'The chapel is on fire, come and help!' brought a crowd, 'with ladders and water'. You can almost feel the panic that gradually gives way to relief as the secretary recorded, 'Messrs. Frederick and Phillip Bath brought their extinguishers and were quickly on the roof with the others...and the fire was put out'. This was, she thankfully records, the second time the chapel had been saved from fire, but 'much damage was done.' There was quite a mess and some damage but once again the church was beautifully cleaned and the restoration was paid for by the insurers.

The Christian life of the church fellowship was full and joyous during these settled days under the new pastor's leadership. He and his wife quickly became friends to all and just as his ministry fostered spiritual growth, also, through his connections, the development of social and artistic intercourse was encouraged.

The visit of Bedford Orpheus Choir and their rendition of Samuel Coleridge Taylor's cantata, 'Hiawatha's Wedding Feast' would have been quite an occasion at the chapel, where the performance of musical scores was appreciated. The choir of Bunyan Meeting, Bedford came to give a Christian performance on another occasion.

Once again 'we are now engaged' in War

So wrote the secretary, opening the minutes of the 1940 annual meeting. This annual meeting, like recent meetings, had been held at Roxton Park, at the invitation of Mr. and Mrs. F. Bath. During the war children from the Hendon area of North London were evacuated to Roxton. The arrival of such a huge influx (the number on the school roll doubled overnight) necessitated many changes and more space had to be found for these pupils and their teachers. During the autumn of 1940 the Chapel Schoolroom was loaned to Bedfordshire County Council and lessons were held there; the groups of local and London children alternated between am and pm in their use of the Chapel. What these Londoners thought about the accommodation, especially the primitive toilets that didn't flush, is a matter for speculation. The original earth closets by this time were *modernised*, having buckets placed below scrubbed pine seats. In the ladies toilet what was called a *two-holer*, a larger and small aperture provided an option for the children. Mr. Leonard their headmaster and the London teachers held meetings in The Chequers P.H. and were responsible for the education and welfare of their charges. Lessons at the chapel only lasted for a short time. Mr. W. Stapleton recalls having lessons in the Park on fine days as at times the older pupils had to remain in the village because no transport was available to take them to the Senior School at Sandy. These young people swelled the congregation throughout their stay.

Mrs Bath, who had suffered a long illness, was now able to take up her role in the work of the church again. Social meetings were curtailed and during the autumn of 1942, afternoon services replaced the evening ones since a "black-out" was enforced; there was, we learn, 'increased night bombing'. In August a donation was sent to the churches of the South and East coasts that had suffered from air-raids and diminishing congregations due to evacuation and collections the following February were to be sent to the Red Cross fund.

Church life continued despite the difficulties. A Jumble Sale had raised £7.10s which was used to buy new floor matting. The children's choir, trained by Mrs. Gilbert and accompanied by Miss. Marjorie King sang beautifully at the Sunday School Anniversary and were rewarded with the customary 'Treat'. (a tea and games in the adjacent Park) A new electric boiler now made tea-making easier and to entertain the children Freddie Bath would pile them on a trailer and take them for a ride to the Roxton woods.

Although in the countryside many carried on their daily lives far removed from the dangers of war, the secretary wrote, 'the year 1940 - the second year of the war has been one of difficulty and anxiety.' Many local men working on the land, were in reserved occupations and so were not *'called up'* to serve king and Country, but most joined the Home Guard and their duties included night shifts on fire - watch at Little Barford Power Station, before they began their day's work. Women had to make ends meet since government legislation had caused the imposition of food and clothing rationing.

The Gift of a New Organ

In April 1941 a splendid gift was delivered and installed in the church. Mr. Phillip Bath procured a two manual, chamber organ that had been built by Bates and Son, of Ludgate Hill, London which had previously been in a private house in Highgate.

This replaced the old harmonium and it was necessary to move the pulpit forward so that the new instrument could be installed against the rear wall of the church. At first the organ had to be pumped by hand. This useful job was done by Freddie Bambridge of Rattlebury Row until an electric blower was installed in 1946.

The organ was dedicated, 'to the Glory of God and the service of this Church,' at a special service held on Sunday April 21st 1942.

Richard Hooker, organist seated at the organ, 2008
S. Gibbs

'The excellence of the new organ' was revealed at the Church Anniversary when Mr. H.J.Colson F.R.C.O. played, '*A Life Laid Down for His Country.*'

How significant that piece of music now seems to have been, since so short a time afterwards, on the first of July 1942, the Rev. Prothero's son lost his life whilst serving his country on H.M.S. Furious whilst in Gibralta harbour. Surgeon Lieutenant D.A. Prothero's life and service to his country are commemorated by a memorial window depicting *The Good Samaritan*, which was placed in the chapel by his parents. The window was unveiled by Mrs. F. Bath at a simple ceremony of dedication which took place on September 27th 1946, just before the termination of Rev. Prothero's ministry. 'The church was filled to overflowing.'

Programme for the Memorial Service and dedication of the Prothero window. Gibbs collection

In 1943 an appeal was launched by the Congregational Union to raise money for damaged churches, called the Restructuring Fund. Roxton Chapel was asked to raise the huge sum of £70.00. Further expense was considered when thoughts turned to how to engage a minister to follow the Rev. Prothero. If a manse was provided it was thought that a retiring minister could be attracted to serve this country church even if the stipend was low. Optimism prevailed and a Manse Fund was set up. During the year it was reported, 'one of our members, Miss Elsie Jefferies has joined the W.R.N.S. The former Sunday School scholar is serving with the forces in Italy.'

Stained Glass Window in memory of Surgeon Lt. D.A.Prothero R.N. 1911-1941

Rev. Prothero served as President of the Beds Union of Baptist and Congregational Churches during the period 1944-5. Many delegates from Roxton had attended his inauguration in Bedford on 14th June.

Roxton members accompanied their Minister, Rev Prothero who was president of the Beds Union during 1944-5
Gibbs collection

A Flying Bomb didn't deter our Minister!

In the winter of 1944 -5 the 'black-out' regulations were revised to 'dim-out' which enabled evening services to be re-started. It was on Sunday 17th December that during the evening service 'we were somewhat alarmed when a flying bomb seemed to pass very low over the chapel,' cutting an overhead cable and plunging the building into darkness. It crashed in a field nearby whilst 'our minister calmly went on with his sermon,' before closing with the benediction. Recalling this, local people tell of the *'Doodlebug'* that flew over the Chapel. It was worrying because the engine had cut out and that meant one thing—it would fall to the ground and explode very soon. 'It came down in Bath's field near the woods - all the lights went out but no damage was caused', it was reported to me some years ago. 'Mr. Prothero carried on preaching and kept everyone calm'. Daylight revealed that it had been a close thing; when passing over the Chapel it had caught the cable and come within a hair's breadth of the main bell turret. Nevertheless there was little other direct proximity to the hostilities; troops moved to and fro on the Great North and Bedford

Roads; Montgomery made an unsolicited stop-over at Park House, and once excited schoolchildren witnessed a dog-fight in the distant sky from the playground.

That year saw the first visit of the Howard Church choir from Bedford, when they sang at the Church Anniversary on May 25th. Mrs Hannah Matthews, widow of the village shepherd and Roxton's oldest resident died on September 3rd 1945 aged 106 years. She had been a Chapel member for forty years.

There was to be no Church Anniversary Tea in 1946 – although the war had ended the previous year. This was unavoidable because of 'the serious food situation'. Rationing was biting, and such commodities as tea and sugar were limited to meagre quantities only available on coupons.

There was shock and sadness when Rev. Prothero announced that he was to terminate his ministry in September 1946. Throughout the previous ten years he and his wife had been devoted to the ministry at Roxton. It was a time that one member (speaking in the 1980's) recalled as 'the happiest time at the Chapel'!

The Bath family were extremely supportive of the Church and Rev. and Mrs. Prothero during his ministry; from left Mr. and Mrs. P. Bath and Mr. and Mrs F. Bath (treasurer).   S. Bath collection

An Era of Change, 1945 -1980

As the country emerged from the war, the familiar rural way of life in the villages seemed hardly to have changed. In Roxton many men who worked small holdings of Market Garden or early cropping land, didn't have the financial ability to mechanise. During the 1940's and 50's horses were still a common sight as they drew ploughs or harrows and carted produce. London markets were accessible by train from Tempsford station and loads of vegetables were also transported by road. Mechanisation was just beginning to spread and on the larger farms as binders and threshing drums gave way to the modern combined harvestors, the Rick Yard (now Southfields) was silenced forever. Building began, which was to change the face of the village, albeit slowly at first. The local authority had provided new homes on two estates, but when the Sunday School children of the 1940's and 1950's were marrying and seeking new homes they were forced to look outside the village to find privately developed property. A generation of young people who had grown up in the Anglican Church or Chapel left the community and most were never to return.

Property development when it came during the 1970's and 1980's attracted new people to live in Roxton. The age of the commuter had arrived, and people had very little time spare at weekends. Gradually throughout the decades the village community has absorbed many new people who have enriched village life, but inevitably the way of life has changed and the old pattern of work and rest that incorporated worship is no more.

The Chapel c 1950   *Gibbs collection*

Whether to provide a Manse?

In 1949 the Manse Fund stood at £580-00. Planning consent was sought from Bedfordshire Rural District Council, to convert part of the building, (possibly the South Wing) into accommodation for a Pastor. P.Bath had instructed E.C.Inskip, Architects to submit plans. However hopes were dashed when the response was received. It indicated that only temporary permission would be granted, and it was realised that the cost couldn't be justified. Plans for the Manse though temporarily shelved, were to lead nowhere.

Mr and Mrs F Bath and Mr. P. Bath in the park. Their support of the church was recognised in the minutes.   S. Bath

Mr & Mrs F. Bath continued in their support for the Church, providing a summer outing to Skegness for the children in 1945 and new Congregational Praise hymn books in 1952; amongst Mr. P. Bath's gifts were the new iron gates. A meeting in 1950 recorded a vote of thanks for the 'very real interest that he has long taken (in the welfare) of our church and his generous help towards the maintenance of the church building.

Ministerial Support from Cambridge Colleges

Students from Cheshunt College Cambridge had come to lead worship throughout the late 1940's and had been entertained by Mr. & Mrs. Bath. Rev.Douglas Smith of Howard Church Bedford, at that time Secretary of the Beds Union of Baptist and Congregational churches, first preached in 1949. He became a friend of the Chapel, the Bath family and a frequent preacher. Other services were led by local preachers including John Brown of Potton and John Cobbold of St. Neots.

Rev Douglas Smith, Howard Congregational Minister
Gibbs collection

For a time, students came from Westminster College and were provided with a meal by church families. Margaret Bambridge deacon said that they mostly travelled to Roxton by 'bus and there was often a hurry to finish singing the last evening hymn so that the student could hurry up the road to the bus-stop in time. On Good Friday 1955 an annual Evening Service of Sacred Music was begun when the Choir from Howard Church, Bedford under the leadership of their conductor, Mr. Gale, gave a performance of John Stainer's *'Crucifixion'*. This accomplished choir with trained soloists continued to minister in choral song every Good Friday for more than twenty-five years; in 1980, sometime after their merger with St.Luke's Church, under the leadership of Keith J. Brown. In 1987, this augmented choir gave a performance of Armstrong Gibbs' 'Behold the Man', when the Potton Salvation Army also joined in creating music for the service.

After the meetings there was always the chapel 'cup of tea'!
May Jefferies, Marjorie Gosling and Marjorie Jarvis.   *The Gosling collection*

In 1956 the deacons met with the deacons of St. Neots Congregational Church and after discussion agreed to link with that church. From that time the St.Neots minister would preach at Roxton once a month officiating at the Communion of the Lord's Supper and having pastoral oversight of the Roxton Fellowship. A financial settlement was agreed between the churches. There followed a settled time with re-assuring ministerial oversight when there was someone to call on for house visits, and to officiate at weddings, baptisms and funerals. Mrs. Gilbert's diary during her declining years indicates how she appreciated the minister's visits, first in 1959, 'Rev Nelson called to see me Feb 3rd and met the doctor.' Then in July 1964, 'Rev. Martin came to see me in Bedford hospital in June' ' Came to see me again at home July 17th'.

The Sunday School and Anniversaries

John King had resigned in 1948 after fifty years as Sunday School Superintendent. The Sunday School Treat was still held in the New Year; in 1948 Mr. E. C. Pearce of Kempston was paid £3. 18s for 'A Magical Entertainment' and Pratt, Bakers and Confectioners of St. Neots provided 66 teas; their bill was £9.18s.

In 1948 and The Sunday School Roll book begins the previous year when 35 children were enrolled; attendance was regular, many coming to chapel twice each Sunday. Some older boys left at that time but in 1948 children from the Bannister, Evans, Cooper, Brace, Darlow, Horner, Meston Gosling Jeffs and Jefferies family joined to keep numbers steady.

Doris Jefferies (who had helped him) and Gertrude Hull carried on the teaching with Mrs D. Chamberlain and Miss S. Bambridge, (the author), helping at various times. During the 1950's an average of thirty children attended the Sunday School. In 1950 a Branch of the Sunday School Union was formed at St. Neots and Roxton affiliated along with local Methodist churches, St. Neots Congregational and Hail Weston Baptists. In 1954 a dedicated team supplied through the St. Neots Sunday School Union which included, Mr.& Mrs. H Cambers, Miss R. Bull and Mr. Madin (who later married), Mr. L. Forscutt and Barbara Forscutt, began to help teach the classes.

The Anniversary was a showcase for the children's talents and advertised locally with posters printed by Thompson & Lendrum, St. Neots. Evening practices were held and Mrs. D. Jefferies coached the children in elocution: clear diction and expression was called for as they practised reciting appropriate verses that

The Jefferies family c 1953 ;
from left Keith, May, William(Bill), J.Thomas, Sarah, K. George, Doris, Rosemary and Trevor.   *Roxton and District Local History Group collection.*

had been learned by heart. Special hymn sheets were bought and George Jefferies played the organ while Mrs E. Gilbert trained the choir and soloists; the Children's Choir seated on the platform to the left of the organ clutched the new hymn-sheets as they practised the unfamiliar tunes. Just how long would the stern-faced Mrs Gilbert, who stood before them, hand beating out the time of the music, persist, they must have wondered. Little did they realise that she had sung in the children's choir herself long ago and been involved with music at the Chapel for over fifty years!

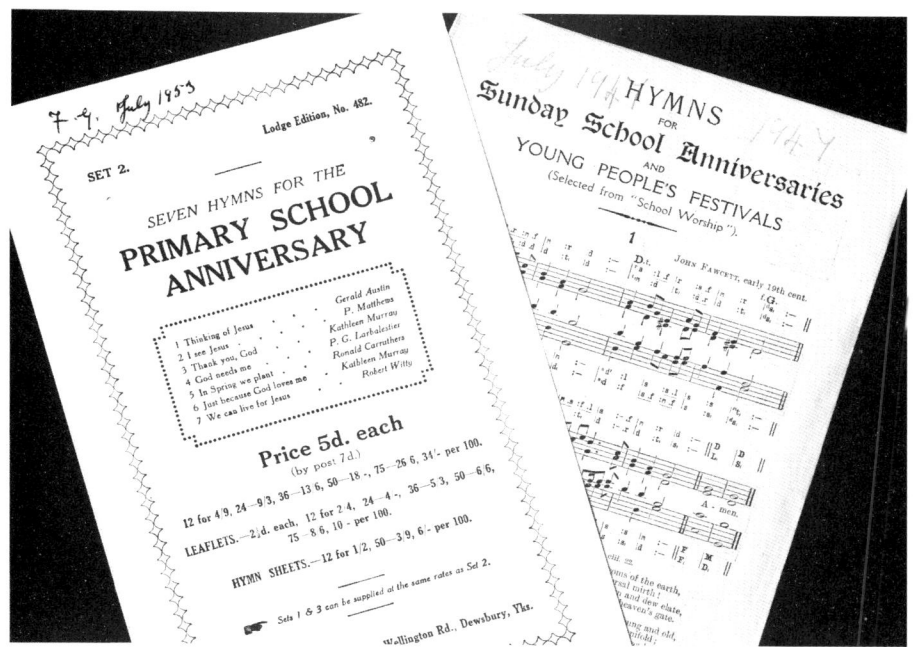

Examples of Sunday School Anniversary Music sheets;   Gibbs collection

On the Day all the pupils wore their *'Sunday Best'* clothes, many of the girls had on a new summer dress as they stood on the platform in readiness. The scholars, faces beaming, confidently rendered recitations, audible despite the nerves which tended to take over on the day; soloists' knees knocked as they climbed the steps to sing from the pulpit to a congregation of proud parents and grandparents and friends who packed the Chapel as the bright singing of the children floated heaven-ward. Mrs Gilbert's diary records, 'July 1952.....I resigned after doing it (rehearsing the choir) for 32 years, 1918-1951.'

ROXTON

ANNIVERSARY. — Large congregations attended the Congregational Church Sunday School anniversary services on Sunday. **The Rev. A. G. Nelson** conducted both afternoon and evening services. He stressed the need for Christian teaching and example in the home. The children sang special hymns and gave a demonstration, "The only way." A recitation was given by **Michael Watson**. Lessons were read by **Rosemary Jefferies, Miss Stella Bambridge** and **Miss Phyllis Chamberlain. Mr. Nelson** congratulated the children on winning the "Farrer" shield in the recent scripture exam., and presented books to the scholars who sat and passed the exam. The children were trained by Miss Phyllis Chamberlain (teacher). Collections for Sunday School funds were £10-13-8. A duet was sung by Miss Stella Bambridge and Miss Marlene Bambridge at the evening service.

A report from the local newspaper about the Sunday School Anniversary

Members and children went to Scripture Union Rallies at St. Neots, and for one week every summer, the travelling Mission pitched a marquee in Chapel Close and held rallies. Village children went to meetings and sang choruses and heard Bible stories. John Walker who was a committed lay preacher dedicated many years to this youth mission work.

Mrs Chamberlain organised a support group for the Sudan. Young people met in her home for prayers, stories of mission work and to make craft items to raise funds.

Craft work on sale in the chapel vestry.   Gosling family collection

From left: Megan Jefferies, Sandra Heckford, Rosemary Jefferies, Diana Cooper, Elizabeth Gosling, Audrey Chamberlain, Anne Darrington?, Brenda Chamberlain, (unknown clergy), Deidre Heckford, (unknown gent)

Sudaneers lead a special service at the Chapel   Gosling family collection
From left; Betty Jarvis, Elizabeth Gosling, Megan Jefferies, Marlene Bambridge, (Unkown Clergy), (unkown), Jean Banister.

The 150th Anniversary

In 1958 during the ministry of Rev. Nelson the church celebrated its 150th year. Special services were held on May 29th when Rev. W. Griffith-Jones, chairman of the Congregational Union of England and Wales preached at an afternoon anniversary service. He extended greetings from the three thousand, nationwide, member churches of the Congregational Union. There were, he said, encouraging 'signs of power and progress in the life of our churches today.' He spoke of increased membership and a rise in numbers coming forward for the ministry. Among the many visitors were Ald. & Mrs. A.A.Jones (Mayor & Mayoress of Bedford) and Rev. T.E.Morris president of the Bedfordshire Union of Baptist and Congregational Churches. Tea, served in the new Parish Hall, concluded the celebrations. Although the weather was wet the chapel was filled to capacity, the local newspaper's reported. The following Sunday celebrations continued with a service led by Rev. Alan Macleod M.A.Professor of Old Testament History at Westminster College, Cambridge.

H.G.Tibbutt, F.R.Hist.S., wrote a history of the church that was published to coincide with the 150th anniversary. The book was a well researched documentation of the history of the Church and was well received. Three hundred copies were printed. Some older members still have a copy and one is held by B.L.A.R.S.

Rev. T. E. Morris, Rev. W. Griffiths Jones, the Mayor and Mayoress of Bedford, A.A. and Mrs Jones,and Rev. Nelson attend the 150th anniversary of the Church from the Bedfordshire Times

The Autumn Meeting of The Beds Union was held at Roxton on Thursday September 25th that year. In anticipation four large teapots had been purchased, and again a tea was held in the new Parish Hall.

Tea was served in the Parish Hall – the Chapel Bone China in use for the dignitaries.
Gibbs collection

Young and old celebrate, still using the fragile china! Mrs Nelson is centre in dark jacket. Gibbs collection *Photographs George Page, St.Neots*

Harvest Festivals

The mid-twentieth century perhaps marked the end of centuries during which generations of Roxton people had lived and worked by the soil. As car ownership became the norm, and people moved to work in towns, a severance from the old affinity with the seasons was taking place. Even as the villagers of the nineteen fifties flocked to sing their harvest praises, filing through the chapel door past harvest sheaves of golden wheat, they marked the passing of a time that is now lost.

They came to see the chapel transformed, swelled gloriously with *God's gifts*. On entry, a profusion of flowers bedecked the interior and a feast of produce ranged on tiered staging in front of the pulpit, while a fusion of wonderful aromas assaulted the nostrils. These laden tables had been arranged by ladies of the church down the years while others fashioned small bunches of wheat. Elsie Brace was known for her wonderful sponge cakes; Fred Gilbert fashioned ropes of his Market-Garden grown Bedfordshire onions and sacks of potatoes from George Bambridge's fields all contributed to the glorious vision of Harvest Home.

F. Gilbert, gardener in the 1950's made a wreath of asters and golden rod that encircled the balcony clock; bunches of grapes hung from the pulpit lectern, and small bunches of wheat, replica sheaves, adorned the finials of the pulpit rail. Harvest hymns raised from crowded pews spelled out the age-old message of reassurance; the affirmation of God's great goodness. These were still the times when older Roxton men worshipped here remembering the felt an affinity to the soil, the last horses that worked the land were still remembered and men went out in all weathers to plough and sow, to mow and ultimately to gather in the harvest.

The Auction of produce

On Monday evening it was a tradition to hold a sale of the harvest produce. More recently gifts of eggs and fruit have been taken to the sick and elderly but at this time the schoolroom was set out with rows of forms and a trestle-table laden with goods; cakes and jams mixed with bunches of carrots, beetroot and ropes of onions alongside the bunches of wheat that would sell as feed for the backyard hens. At seven p.m. everyone stood and waited for the proceedings to begin. Goods were held up for auction and offers ran up as the skilful auctioneer pitted one bidder against another. Some bargains were had but all entered into the spirit of fund-raising with generosity, and went home having thoroughly enjoyed the evening. Tommy Harpur once bought a brood of

Harvest Display about 1900
Gibbs collection

Harvest Display 2007.   S.Gibbs

Chickens that was auctioned – but on this occasion they weren't taken to the chapel! During the Years when the Steam Engine Rally was held in Roxton Park (1969-1993), women who stayed on site in their caravans swelled the numbers at the sale. Then bidding was even brisker, and a healthy competitive atmosphere prevailed. Some auctioneers remembered are Phillip Bath, Hugh Careless, J. (Jim) Bambridge, Louis Livett, and W.(Bill) Robinson. It was customary to send a donation from the proceeds to Bedford hospital.

"Didn't We Have a Lovely Time" on the Chapel Outings!

Summer outings were started earlier in the twentieth century but no records remain. Begun as a trip to Wicksteed Park, later a day at the sea which evolved from the former *Sunday School Treats*. These proved to be very popular village '*outings*' since not every family could afford a summer holiday during the 1950's and a day out with sandwiches and flasks, towels, buckets and spades was something to look forward to for the whole family. Trips to Skegness, Clacton, and Hunstanton were enjoyed. In 1950 we travelled by *Baxter's Luxury Coaches of Moggerhanger,* when two coaches charged at £30.00, ran to Skegness. Then in 1952, two twenty-three seater and one thirty-three seater coaches supplied by L. Safford and son, Gt. Gransden at a cost of £36.00 took us to Hunstanton. Many of today's grandparents will recall joining in singing, *She'll be Coming Round the Mountain When She Comes,* and other popular songs on the journey home! Sand-garnished cheese and tomato sandwiches have never tasted better since!

Fred and Elsie Brace on a Chapel Outing
Gibbs collection

Larkinson's in St. Neots was the shop that stocked everything for the child in the 1950's and they supplied suitable items for Sunday School Christmas party presents. In 1952, £1-8-9 was spent on items that included; Ludo, Blow Football, an album, and a money box. Gordon Jefferies received a knife (*no-one had heard of political correctness in those days*), Trevor Jefferies a train and Keith Jefferies a spinning top. Girls were given hankies, hair brushes and books.

The Great Big Garden Tidy Up!

John Gibbs, Keith Jefferies and Tom Bambridge tidy near the old pond some time before the garden was cleared and the pond filled   *Gibbs collection*

In the 1960's the garden was made considerably easier to manage when Mr. P. Bath arranged for his workmen to clear away unsightly bushes around the rear and southern side of the plot. The area was tidied, the old dried pond was filled and levelled and a new railing fence was erected. At the time a wheel of the tractor apparently dropped into a hole and the workmen thought the hole discovered might be a small vault, created when the barn had been transformed into a chapel so long ago. Since this posed a danger, for safety it was filled in and the ground levelled over.

In 1961 water was laid on at the building, enabling flush toilets to be installed in the Northern wing later in 1969. It was in 1961 that the building was treated for a serious infestation of beetle and woodworm that was posing a major threat. For years afterwards the chemical smell pervaded the building, but after destruction of badly infested furniture from the schoolroom the problem was eradicated.

The first Carol Service was held in December 1955: it was both a celebration of the Birth of the Christ Child and a way of raising funds for the *National Children's Home*, a practice that continues today, under the guise of the modern name *N.C.H. for Children*.

The Decision to Remain an Independent Congregational Church

Rev. Nelson's ministry concluded in 1963 when he moved to a church in Seaton, Devon. Then in 1965 consideration was given to a proposal that Roxton join with the St. Neots and Potton churches in venture to share a minister. This was eventually rejected and the previous arrangement with St. Neots continued. He was succeeded by Rev. R. Martin who ministered here from 1964-1969; and then Rev. J. Hickmore was minister from 1969-1977. During Rev. Hickmore's ministry, in 1971 the Congregational Church proposed a link with the Presbyterian Church. The new church was to be known as the United Reformed Church. Each church was asked to discuss the proposal fully and then members were asked to vote on the merger at a special meeting. At Roxton the vote to reject the merger was unanimous. Other churches, including our sister fellowship at St. Neots went ahead on a majority, Roxton Chapel remained within the Congregational denomination. Some years later the Federation could not find the deeds of our Chapel, realising they had been missing for many years. Eventually they were located, having been transferred with those of other churches, into the hands of the United Reformed Church!

Long time servants of our Church, George and Doris Jefferies left the village for Bedford in 1967. George, farmer and trained horticulturalist had been a long-time chapel gardener keeping the lawns and grounds in good order. He is remembered for the skill and dedication with which he nurtured the lovely rose bed, which blooms gloriously each summer to this day, tended by a new generation of gardeners all of whom work long hours for the glory of God.

Another who like them would be sorely missed, Annie Florence Bath, died in 1968. Among the Lay Preachers mentioned who helped lead our worship during the 1970's are John Cobbold, John Davey and David Bushby.

Roxton Farm Grows Straw to Re-thatch the Roof.

Throughout the mid-nineteenth century the thatched roof had been patched and the ridge had been repaired, but by the late 1960's it was obvious that a complete re-thatch was necessary. Mr. Bath agreed to grow wheat especially for the thatch on his farm. An older variety was selected, since wheat grown at that time had been developed with shorter *straw* ie. Stems. When harvested, the special wheat gave long sturdy straw, and Mr. Tomkins, thatcher from Willington carried out the work in 1971 at the cost of £1054. A November sale of work raised £74 'for the thatching' and an April Jumble sale £40, but in 1972 a note stated, '£150 still owed on the thatching.' It had been an expensive decade. But the straw was to be very durable and lasted over twenty years. The external repainting was completed in 1976 at a cost of £354.

Early 1970's Wedding Party in the grounds – thatching was carried out in 1971
B. Hooker collection

Annual Jumble sales with an auction, and sales of work, raised encouraging sums that offset such expenses during this period, while gift money towards the purchase of a new carpet was received from the village Friendly Circle. A decade later the Flower Show committee gave £100 towards the cost of rewiring the building.

The Sunday School children excelled at their Scripture examinations in 1961 winning the Farrer Shield that year. In 1962 numbers had dropped to 13, with the last to register being Tina Livett, Sheila Gosling and Jane and Carol Robinson, but numbers in attendance declined thereafter, and the Sunday School closed for several years in 1969 when Miss Hull retired. In 1978 it was successfully re-started under the tutorage of Mrs. Jean Lucas, and Mrs Joyce Hooker with support from Rev. Trice who came from St. Neots to help. The influx of thirty children of a new generation attended regularly and particularly enjoyed the Christmas trips to the pantomime.

Although reduced in number, steadfast Christians continued the work for Christ at Roxton, with a few taking on the workload that had in the past been borne by so many. However church records show that between 1959 and 1964 sixteen new members had joined the Church fellowship.

Deacons c.1960 from left; K.G.Jefferies, J.T.Jefferies, Rev. Nelson, F. Darrington, G.T.Bambridge.

Photograph G. Page Gibbs collection

Shared Fellowship and new friends from St. Neots and Potton Friends

It was on Good Friday in 1974 that the first visit of Potton Salvation Army Band is recorded in the church book. The story of Christ's Passion was told through their skills as musicians and songsters as they preached the Gospel in their own special way. In the 1950's members travelled to St. Neots to join in worship. Mrs. Gilbert's diary reads, 'March 17th 1953 Fred and I with Mrs. Jefferies and George went to St. Neots Congregational to hear Rev. Tizard of Birmingham at 4 o'clock Service and tea and stayed to 7 o'clock service. Came home by taxi.' Contact between the fellowships strengthened as a natural outcome of sharing ministers. The diary continues, 'went to St. Neots Cong. Church by Bus, June 6th 1965-no service at Roxton Chapel'. It was during these years lasting Christian friendships that have enriched the lives of members of both these Christian fellowships were forged.

The Chapel looking beautiful in the snow

B. Hooker collection

The Closing years of the Millennium.

Although congregations had declined by the 1980's loyal members worked to maintain regular worship and a historic building. The pattern of many young members leaving to go to college or university coupled with deaths of older members meant that inevitably support for the church lessened. Having lost potential younger members it seemed that the general pattern of decline in membership recognised in the wider church, and reflected here, lay in the sweeping changes that were occurring in society as a whole. Increased leisure activities including sporting activities, Sunday opening hours for shops, and the availability of cheap travel were among the forces of change happening in society difficulty at that time that caused a disinclination of people in shifting populations to commit to regular Church attendance. Additionally worship and the relevance of and practice of religion were increasingly questioned in the new secular age.

Nevertheless, because it is such an appealing building Roxton Chapel continued to be a focus of attention, which served to draw attention to Christian worship through different media. Throughout the last century it had featured in several local publications both newspapers and magazines, and in 1995, it was included in the Anglia Television programme *'Timpson's Country Churches'* hosted by the former Radio Four *Today* presenter, John Timpson. The series which featured churches throughout East Anglia, was filmed on location with John Timpson travelling from church to church in an old Morris Traveller. Roxton Chapel was included in the fifth of the six programmes with seven other churches in Bedfordshire, Buckinghamshire and Hertfordshire. An accompanying booklet was published. The Chapel also featured on Anglia Television's regular feature *Unique Properties* sometime in the 1990's.

Although congregations had been few in number, at times publicity and visits with guided tours arranged by Bernard Hooker had brought new friends to worship at the church. Throughout these years he and his wife had welcomed visitors, given slide presentations and tours; friends from Millfield Congregational Church, Peterborough and Park Road Methodist Church Bedford, as well as women's groups and local history groups, had been among the visitors. Numbers in the weekly congregation have grown slowly since this time.

After Rev. Sam Madin left the St. Neots church in 1997 it was no longer possible to arrange for their minister, who was then serving reduced hours, to have ministerial oversight for the church at Roxton. Churches were moving into a period when they needed to rely more on lay preachers once again.

The Church at Roxton has truly been fortunate in retaining a supply of such committed preachers over many years, and we find that as one becomes unable to continue, then we are blessed with another. Ministers from nearby Congregational churches help by officiating at marriages, funerals and baptisms and we are grateful to Rev. Colin Price from Guilden Morden, Rev. Angus Mc Cormack from Shillington and Rev. Chris Damp from Bunyan Meeting for their support at these and other important services. They and other ordained clergy led the offices of the sacrament monthly.

In 1990, when Marjorie Gosling who had faithfully served as organist for so many years, retired due to failing health, it seemed that the time had come to face singing unaccompanied. It was then that Richard Hooker courageously set about learning to play the organ. Having sung the hymns for many years he practised hard and this self-taught accompanist now plays with skill and confidence at most services. Steve Eldridge helps occasionally as do visiting organists. We are also fortunate to be able to call on Graham Westcott of Gt. Staughton to play for very special occasions.

Monthly Coffee Mornings and Evenings became popular social occasions which were supported by so many from the village and wider church community. These coffee mornings, begun in the 1980's were important to fund raising, and helpers were abundant.

Ladies prepare stalls for the monthly coffee mornings   *B. Hooker collection*

Coffee mornings helped to raise funds; customers pause in the chapel for the opening prayer. B. Hooker collection

The cake stall was laden with delicious cakes, and crafts filled another stall. Bric-a-Brac and White Elephants came out of the cupboards and a good chat was enjoyed over coffee and scones. Amongst the many contributors Marjorie Gosling, Gwen Gadsden and Lily Wildman were skilled bakers; Lily Wildman and Stella Gibbs worked to make crafts and Joyce Hooker and Margaret Bambridge turned their hands to make mouth-watering cakes and scones. The minutes tell this event, 'brought many new people into the Church.' Rev. Keith Trice attended the early coffee mornings to open the meeting with prayer, and the deacons continue this practice today. Coffee mornings took on a new importance when funds were needed urgently.

The life of the Church community was enriched through association with other Christians; regular exchanges occurred with St, Neots U.R.C. for anniversaries, flower festivals and special services, and they joined in an annual Summer outing and a Sunday picnic before evening worship. The West Anglia Gospel Choir and the Potton Salvation Army and Songsters led Christian praise services annually. For several years during the 1990's the Good Friday choral tradition was upheld; the Upper Room ecumenical choral group from St.Neots giving a presentation of the Easter story through dramatic readings by David Bushby, and accompanying music.

*Deacon Jean Lucas
arranging flowers
in the church
B. Hooker collection*

Friends from St. Mary Magdalene, Roxton joined in fellowship for a United Carol Service from the 1990's and in turn Chapel members worshipped on various occasions with them.

The Chapel outing continued through these years often the coach taking members and friends to Hunstanton for the day. With decreasing support it was discontinued in 2000, the last outing having been the previous Summer to Gt. Yarmouth.

*Since the 1980's friends from St. Neots U.R.C. have joined in summer picnic
followed by worship. B. Hooker collection*

The Major Restoration of this Historic Building

It was during 1984 that Deacon George Bambridge became concerned about the deteriorating state of the thatched roof, in particular the north side of the building seemed to be in a very poor state. In his opinion, patching and rewiring was urgently needed. Estimates in the region of £4,000 came in for the work. Alarmingly this amount was more than could be afforded at this time, and the deacons met to reconsider. Since the building was listed grade two starred, English Heritage were approached for assistance, and thereafter a restoration project, the enormity of which the deacons could never have envisaged, was begun.

An important meeting called early in 1990 was attended by Mr. B. Hart a senior partner in the Bedford firm of Inskip & Son., who was appointed to act as architect for the Church; Mrs. Betty Swarbrick from the Congregational Federation, a representative from English Heritage, and a surveyor of historic churches who was there to inspect and advise. He stated that the building 'was well worth restoring for future generations'. The next step was to obtain estimates for the necessary work. It came as an horrific shock when the figure of £93,000 was arrived at; that being to cover the main elements of the work on the structure and complete re-roofing. This would still leave much cosmetic work to be done.

How could the work be funded?

Although an application for grant aid was immediately submitted to English Heritage such matters are inclined to be protracted, grant bodies allocate money from annual budgets and then delays are caused until the next annual tranche of money becomes available. Meanwhile the roof was deteriorating further.

English Heritage awarded 70% of the estimated cost, leaving the Church to 'find' the balance. It was, suggests Bernard Hooker, treasurer, something of what, as Believers, we may call 'the hand of God' that moved in our favour. It was essential to begin the work rapidly—the roof was no longer sound, but further delay was expected since thatchers always have a backlog of work. However, when in the 1980's property prices collapsed, some contracts were cancelled or delayed, thus enabling Mr. P. Lewis, Master Thatcher to finalise with a more competitive price and begin the work sooner.

The whole restoration project was overseen by both Mr. Hart, architect appointed for the Church and Mr. V. Farrer architect acting for English Heritage.

Reed was specified for the thatch, it being more durable than straw and more suited to the style of building. The shallow gradient of the roof causes it to drain less well and reed thatch in the past had lasted well. The work went ahead, and the roof and exterior decor was completed by June 1994. With further money that the church members had raised and generous grant help from many charitable bodies, it was possible to replace decayed timber around the building and completely redecorate both internally as well as externally.

Thatching in progress on the Southern side.
All from the B Hooker collection

When the old thatch was stripped it was evident that much roof timber on the North wing had to be replaced, as did a massive oak beam that supported the main North wall of the building. Due to rot in this support over many decades, the whole side of the building had settled, causing the balcony to drop also. New timbers of air dried oak for the North roof alone cost £8000! A *French Drain* was put beside the North wall to take water away from the foundations. The administration of this complex task was overseen by Mr. Bernard Hooker who, deploying expertise gained from his employment, took over this responsibility from Mrs. Bambridge the Church Secretary. The entire project was successfully completed in 1998 and the building once again looked as it would have done when Mr. Metcalfe's builders had fashioned it from a barn nearly two-hundred years earlier.

Timber and foundations had rotted and are being replaced on the Northern side of the building.

Rotten roof timbers were replaced on the Northern side

Thatching on the back (Western) side progressing

It was early in the 1990's that a decision to join the Congregational Federation had been taken, after considerable advice from Rev. J. Franks. Following this the Congregational Federation Ltd. was vested with the trusteeship of the building. Mr. G. T. Bambridge who had first raised concern about the state of the building was sadly not to see the work even begun; after 31 years devoted service to the Church in the various capacities of deacon, secretary and treasurer he passed away in June 1985. His wife Margaret, also a deacon, set about taking over his duties as secretary and served in that capacity until Mr. B. Hooker, her son in law began to help with the workload.

In 1994 when the restoration was nearing completion the Church hosted the *Autumn Assembly* of the East Midlands Region of the Congregational Federation. Many delegates came from member churches spread throughout the region and a united afternoon service was held after which tea was served in the Parish Hall The meeting focussed interest on our church from fellow Congregationalists and brought many numbers of visitors.

The Chapel bell was in need of a new bell rope had been silenced for a number of years. Finally the considerable cost could be met and at last it rang its rather melancholy tone again to call people to worship.

Fellowship is regularly shared with St. Mary's Church; here tea is served after a Carol Serrvice in the 1990's.   B. Hooker collection

Dedication of the Bath Memorial Window

A service of thanksgiving for the completion of the restoration was held in June 1998. During this service a new stained glass window given by Mrs. June Bath in memory of her husband and church supporter, Mr. Phillip Charles Bath was dedicated. The window, which depicts St. Francis, is situated behind the Bath pew which has been reserved through two hundred years for the successive families who have resided in Roxton House. This window was designed and made in the workshops of Goddard and Gibbs the East London stained glass specialist company who made the Prothero memorial window in 1946.

This company, founded in 1868 have built up a reputation for specialising in restoration of period traditional stained glass windows as well as the skilled design and manufacture of new commissions. Their two specialist studio designers 'have over 60 years of experience in the design and making of stained glass between them'. The company has many prestigious works in this country to its credit. They also work with different cultures, carrying out commissions worldwide. At the time this window was made we understand that some of the work was carried out by a craftsman who had also worked on the Prothero window fifty or so years previously.

Memorial window to Phillip Charles Bath 1911-1989, dedicated 1998
S. Eldridge

Into the 21st Century

We are fortunate that during recent years new friends have come to worship regularly at the Chapel and it is encouraging that some young families have joined our fellowship. Some children that have been baptised in recent years are being involved in the church community.

Nicola Eldridge with parents Steven and Kate Eldridge, 2nd September 2001

S. Eldridge

Charles Alexander with parents James and Erica Young, and Rev. L. Albone, 17th July 2005

J. Young

Lilah Koehler with parent Erica Young, baptised 13th May 2007; also from left T. Pike, J. Hooker, R. Hooker, B. Hooker, J. Pike and M. Bambridge

J. Young

John Gibbs serving on RNLI stall   B. Hooker

Christmas Stalls, from left, Mrs. J. Hooker, Mrs. S. Gibbs, Mr. T. Pike and Mrs. I. O'Dell
B. Hooker

To mark the Millennium a *Good News* Bible was purchased for the pulpit.

The Church has been opened to the wider community through new village initiatives. Open gardens begun in 2003 have brought many visitors who have toured the building before enjoying tea in the gardens. An Open Garden event is planned for early summer 2008. Coffee mornings and other events attract many new people into the Church. Harvest Festivals and Carol Services in recent years have been occasions when so many from the community have joined in praise and worship and the chapel has been filled as it would have been many years ago.

The members meet and worship on special occasions at other local Congregational Churches and regularly join in worship with St. Neots United Reformed Church and St. Mary Magdalene, Roxton. Rev. Barbara Ebeling, vicar and Brenda Jennings, Reader are among the many who have regularly conducted services at the Chapel. Dedicated deacons have oversight of the running of the Church, and Margaret Bambridge, a member for sixty-three years, has served for many as a deacon, church secretary from 1985-1994 and was made honorary life-deacon in 2005.

The congregation after the service on Sunday March 9th 2008   S. Eldridge

In March 2002 the Church hosted the Spring Meeting of the East Midlands area of the Congregational Federation. Delegates from many churches, some as far away as Leicester, Market Harborough and Nottingham and Northampton attended and after the service enjoyed tea in the Parish Hall. Roxton has been nominated by the executive to be Church of the Year, in the East Midlands Area of the Congregational Federation in 2008 and will host the area meeting in September. In the meantime plans are well underway for the very special Bicentennial Celebrations at the end of May and first day of June 2008. An open afternoon with garden teas is planned for Saturday followed by a service of thanksgiving conducted by Rev. Chris Damp of Bunyan Meeting Church, Bedford on Sunday 1st June. Afternoon tea will then be served in the Parish Hall.

Once again the building needs repairs and restoration; the thatch completed in 1994 has not been as durable as might have been expected and generous grant aid has been secured to preserve this Grade 11* listed building into the future.

Loyal deacons work devotedly to keep the Church running and to ensure that worship may continue here. We are aware that we are custodians of a beautiful historic building. No-one can tell how old the main part of the building must be; cattle sheltered here in the old barn 'in the occupation of William Brown' and hay was stored here beside the village pasture long before the church was conceived. We step back in time as we enter the ancient building, just as we gaze metaphorically back to a bygone age through the pages of this history. We trust that God will continue to work through us in this place. We cannot know how long worship will continue in this building, for, like the founders of this Church we cannot divine God's great plan for the work of His people here.

We simply hand the future of this fellowship back to God, re-affirming the commitment made by those who founded the Church two-hundred years ago;

'That we .... humbly hoping that we have received the Grace of God in truth .... do resolve this day .... henceforth to walk together as long as circumstances shall permit in the fellowship of the Gospel'

The Deacons March 2008 - B. Hooker, M.Bambridge, J.Hooker, S. Gibbs

Bi-centennial Postscript

As we assemble from diverse places and many churches to mark the bi-centenary of our church and give thanks for two hundred years of Christian Witness at Roxton, we think not only of the past but look with God's help to the future. Let us seek to apply what has been preached and learned through many generations of Christian worship in this place.

Like all histories this book documents times of joy in shared fellowship, tempered by times of great difficulty both for individuals, families and the Christian community here in Roxton. Generations come and go like straws in the wind of time and as we have seen many have made a lasting mark. Others, un-named here are known exclusively to their Heavenly Father, and are recognised no less since they saw it their Christian duty to support the work of spreading God's word here; no less thought of they who quietly arranged fresh flowers, clipped the hedge, stoked the old boiler, trimmed oil lamp wicks, polished brass door knobs or wound the clock.

Step into this church and admittedly one steps back in time to a bygone age. Perhaps the unchanged building; although discreetly succumbing to electric light and heating, running water and plumbing, with its simple interior, offers something unique to the 'weary and heavy-laden' of the 21st Century. Here peace and tranquility can be found; a place where despite the proximity to busy roads, the modern world can seem far away and God's restorative peace may be felt even by those who do not specifically seek it.

Appendix 1
Pastors and Ministers to
Roxton Congregational Church 1808-2008

1808 -1823	No Pastor: Charles James Metcalfe Esq. and other local preachers
1824-1831	Rev. Thomas Nottage
1831-1851	Rev. Henry Winzar
1851-1860	No settled pastor. Students from Cotton End Congregational Academy helped, including Joseph Williams (Dec.1853-Dec.1854); Stephen Bater (Jan.-June 1855)
1860-1872	Rev. John William Rolls
1873-1877	Rev. James Gunn
1886-1908	Thomas Chapman; a lay preacher from St. Neots
1909-1913	Rev. James Hammil
1914-1924	Rev. Richard Harmstone B.A.
1925-1933	Rev. Ernest Slater
1934-1935	Rev. Alfred Norman Rowland M.A.
1936-1947	Rev. David Prothero, B.A., B.D., B.Sc.
1947-1956	Support from Bedford Bunyan Meeting Pastors and Rev.Douglas Smith, Howard Church, Bedford. Theological students from Cheshunt and then Westminster Colleges Cambridge regularly led Sunday evening worship. Local lay preachers also supplied.
1957-1963	Rev. A.G.Nelson
1964-1969	Rev. R.S.Martin
1970-1977	Rev. John Hickmore
1978-1983	Rev. Keith Trice
1985-1997	Rev. Sam Madin
1997-2008	No settled pastor or regular pastoral oversight but local Congregational Ministers conducted baptisms, weddings and funeral services. They and ministers from other denominations officiated at the Communion of the Lord's Supper.

Appendix 2

'**We are called to be Angels; to do God's work for a time. Each generation of Christians then hands on the best of what they have done to others who have been called to follow them.**' Rev. Dr. Alan Argent, Bunyan Meeting Church, Bedford Sunday 24th Feb. 2008.

Charles James Metcalfe: Deacon 1824 -1850

Charles Metcalfe Jnr.: Deacon 1848-1850

Jabez Hawkins; Assistant Preacher -1848

Hugh Bentley: Deacon 1853

John Newling: Deacon 1834-1858

Thomas Newling: Deacon 1858

James Bond, possibly Snr.: Librarian Mid 1800's; Deacon 1862-1869

William Bainbridge: Deacon 1872

Cornelius Darrington: Deacon 1872

Mrs. Brace: Caretaker 1902-1920

James Bond; possibly Jnr.: Deacon -1904; Sunday School Superintendent -1904.

James Day: Financial Deacon 1905

John King: Deacon 1905-1948; Treasurer 1908-1917; Sunday School Superintendent 1948

Thomas Gilbert: Deacon 1905- 1924; Sunday School Teacher 1905-1945; Treasurer 1917

William George Simcoe: Choirmaster 1907-1917

John Thomas Jefferies: Deacon 1916- 1924; Church Secretary from 1918-1920

Albert Ekins: Church Secretary 1904, 1915-1924 ; Choirmaster 1917 -

Caleb Covington: Deacon 1905; Sunday School Superintendent 1915; Gardener 1913-1916

Kitty Ekins: Organist from 1917

Mrs King: Organist -1917

Mrs. Sarah Jefferies: Organist c1920-

Mrs. Lydia Livett: Caretaker 1922-

Miss. Gertrude Hull: Organist c.1922-1950's; Sunday School Superintendent 1950 -1969; Missionary Secretary 1940 -1969

Thomas Harpur: Deacon 1923

Alfred King: Deacon 1924

Miss. Edith E. King: Organist c.1920; Deacon 1924 - 1942; Church Secretary 1925- 1942

Mrs. Annie Florence Bath: Deacon 1935-; Treasurer 1925-1951 and 1962

Miss Marjorie King (Mrs. P. Gosling): Organist 1926- 1940; 1961; 1979-1990

Mrs E. Gilbert; Choirleader 1922-1952

Mrs. G. Jeffs: Deacon 1935; Sunday School Teacher 1948

Miss. Nancy Holden: Deacon 1935-

Mr. J. King: Deacon 1935-

Kenneth George Jefferies: Junior Assistant Organist c.1924; Organist c. 1930-1967; Deacon 1935-1962; Treasurer & Church Secretary 1945 -1962; Gardener -1967

Frank Darrington: Band of Hope Treasurer c.1920 -30's; Deacon 1930's-1978; Leader Sunday Morning Worship 1945-1962 Mrs. Doris Jefferies: Sunday School Superintendant 1940's

Frederick Gilbert: Deacon 1944: Gardener 1917-1957

Mr. & Mrs T. Jefferies: Caretakers 1930's -1950's

Mrs Elsie Brace: Assistant Caretaker 1944

Rev. Prothero: Church Secretary 1944 -1946

Mrs. Dora Chamberlain: Sunday School Teacher 1951-1953

George Jeffs: Deacon 1951

Philip Gosling: Deacon 1951; Treasurer 1951

Teachers from St. Neots Sunday School Union: 1954

Mrs S. Gibbs (Bambridge): Infant Sunday School Teacher 1955-1958; deacon 2003-serving 2008

Mrs. Hearne: Secretary Friday Fellowship 1958-1961

Trevor Jefferies: Church Secretary1958

George Thomas Bambridge: Deacon 1955-1985; Gardener 1960-1985 ; Church Secretary 1962-1985; Treasurer 1963

Louis Livett: Deacon 1956 -19; Assistant Gardener c.1970-80

Mrs.Margaret Bambridge: Deacon1955; Church Secretary 1985; Hon. Life Deacon 2005, serving2008.

George A. Bambridge; Assistant Gardener c1960

Ian Gosling: Deacon 1968-1992; Treasurer 1968-1988

William Robinson: Deacon 1974-1988

Bernard Hooker; Deacon 1986; Treasurer 1993; Gardener 1980's, serving in all 2008

Mrs. Jean Lucas: Sunday School Leader 1978-1987; Deacon 1986; Treasurer 1988-1993; Marriage Acts Nominee 1983-1985

Mrs. Joyce Hooker: Sunday School Teacher/ Treasurer 1978-1987; Deacon 1979-serving 2008

Richard Hooker: Organist 1990-serving 2008; Assistant Gardener c.1990-serving 2008

Steven Eldridge: Assistant Organist 1995-serving 2008

Appendix 3

Some Marriages Celebrated at Roxton Chapel

Sydney George Gadsden and Gwendoline Doris Livett
October 28th 1938

Fred Gilbert and Susan Elizabeth Simcoe, December 18th 1912
deacon, gardener; choirleader

George Thomas Bambridge and Margaret Ann Pike
December 27th 1943
treasurer, secretary ; secretary and life deacon

Geoffrey Alan Livett and
Doreen May Horner
March 26th 1960,
Louis Livett, (deacon) on left.
(George Page, St. Neots.)

John Ernest Gibbs and Stella Joan Bambridge, deacon, September 1st 1962

Bernard George Hooker and Joyce Ann Bambridge, October 9th 1965 Deacon, Treasurer, correspondence secretary; deacon (Walter E Graves, Bedford)

Robert Anthony Street and Angela Bath, August 28th 1971

Tina Elizabeth Livett and David Jones Paine, September 24th 1983

James Alexander Young and
Erica Francesca Koehler,
August 23rd 2003

Ian Phillip Gosling and
Eileen May Priest,
June 6th 1987
Marjorie and Phillip Gosling;
organist ; treasurer

Richard Lewin Haines
and Christine Bath,
June 25th 1994

James Stewart Gordon and Annabel
Clare Bradley, July 26th 2003;
(Nicholas Harvey)

Alan John Fox and Emma Louise Lucas,
September 3rd 1994;
(Simon Ellis, Brampton.)

Index

Anglican Church; 5,13,18,37-8
Argent. Rev. Dr. Alan; 131
Band of Hope; 69,83
Bates & Son, Ludgate Hill, London, Organ builders; 91
Bedford Academy at Bunyan Meeting; 45
Bedford Sunday School Union; 61,63,84
Bedford Modern School; 88
Bedford Orpheus Choir; 90
Bedford Polychordia; 88
Bedfordshire Union of Christians, (The Bedfordshire Union of Baptist and Congregational Churches); 1,11,14,19,22,28, 50,55,61,63,65,69-70,73,80,86,88,94,98,104-5
Berridge. Rev. John; 13
Bonsall. Rev. D.S.; 83
Brown. Rev. John. B.A., D.D.; 13-14,19,29,45,52
Bunyan Meeting Free Church, Bedford; 13-22, 31,45,65,87-90,116,128
Chapman. Thomas; 48-65,71
Chawston; 5,38,50,
Cheshunt College, Cambridge; 69,98
Congregational Home Missionary Society; 45
Congregationalism /Congregational Union of England and Wales/Congregational Federation; 21,31,80,89,92,110,119,122-3,128
Cotton End Academy; 44-45,46
Countess of Huntingdon; 79
Damp. Rev. Chris J. M.A.,B.D.; 116,128
Delap. Major Robert; 44,70,8
Evacuation, WW11; 90
Farringdon. Marianne; 81
Fordham, Cambridgeshire; 5-6
Greethead. Rev. Samuel; 14
Gilbert Family; 59
Goddard and Gibbs, stained glass designers and manufacturers; 93,123,124
Griffiths-Jones. Rev. W.; 104
Harmstone. Rev. Richard. B.A.; 69-79
Hillyard. Rev. Samuel; 14,19,22

Highbury College; 30
Horley. Bishop; 14-5
Howard Congregational Church, Bedford; 31,95,98
League of Nations; 83
Leigh. Sir Eggerton; 14
Livett Family; 60
London Missionary Society; 14,21,45,81
Macleod. Rev Alan; 104
Matthews. Rev Timothy; 13
Morell. Rev. Thomas; 10-11,19,22,24
Morris. Rev. T.E.; 104
Newport Pagnell Theological College; 22
Nottage. Rev. Thomas; 22-28
Parker-Bull. Rev. Thomas; 22
Potton; 65,(Salvation Army); 113,117
Price. Rev. Colin. B.A., M.Phil.; 116
Prothero. Rev David. B.A., B.D., B.Sc.; 87-95
Roll of Honour; 74-5
Rolls. Rev. John William; 46,48
Rowland. Rev. A.N., M.A.; 86,87
Saint Luke's Church, Bedford; 98
Salvation Army; 79,113
St. Mary Magdalene, Roxton; 46,55,58,69,79, 115,118,123,127
Slater. Rev.; 80-86
Smith. Rev. Douglas; 98
Stevens. Rev. W.; 19
St. Neots Old Meeting, (St. Neots Congregational/United Reformed Church); 9-11,19-20,34,99,110,112-3,117,127
St.Neots Sunday School Union; 100,102,112
Tibutt. H.G. F.R. Hist. Soc.; 1,47,61,104
Trinity College, Cambridge; 6
Trinity College, Oxford; 6
Wesley. Charles; 13-14
Westminster College, Cambridge; 98,104
Wymondley College, Hertfordshire; 11,19, 22,30
Winzar. Rev. Henry; 30-42